Poetry, Stories, Questions and Prompts
for Your Faith Journey

Let Your

GIFTS

Shine Forth

Alma L. Carr-Jones

Paperback ISBN-13: 978-1-948026-90-1
Digital ISBN-13: 978-1-948026-91-8
Workbook ISBN-13: 978-1-948026-92-5

Published by TMP Books, 3 Central Plaza Ste 307, Rome, GA 30161
www.TMPBooks.com

Dedicated to

Preachers' Wives Everywhere

To my FATHER, The GOD of Romans 8:28
by Whom I understand the above Scripture to mean that
"Though all things that happen to me
may not be my doing or to my liking,
He makes all of these things
work out for my betterment (growth)
and ultimately, my good!"

To the starry-eyed child who still dwells within - To Excelsior

To Lula M. Peters-Carr, My Momma (R.I.P.)

Oh Great FATHER of Mine
(Song)

Oh great FATHER of mine
Thou has been wowing mankind
Since the beginning of time.
I'm praising in appreciation with humble submission
Thanking You, LORD, that some
Of the awe is mine.

(Refrain): Uhm-m-m FATHER W-O-O-O-W!
I thank You
I bless You
LO-O-R-RD, I'm thankful
For the privilege of prayer
Uhm-m-m, I'm thankful
W-O-O-O-W
To be a child of THINE!

Being blessed with the privilege of prayer
Along with the rest of mankind
Am so thankful to be acknowledged
As a child of THINE
And I praise You
I bless You for
Accepting praise from me
Though You are divine.

The psalmist wrote in Psalms 65
Of his being inspired and wowed
Way back in Biblical times
But I am humbled and grateful that You
Let your glory come shining through
By allowing this "earthen vessel" to be a conduit too!

(Refrain): Uhm-m-m FATHER W-O-O-O-W!
I thank You

I bless You
LO-O-R-RD, I'm thankful
For the privilege of prayer
Uhm-m-m, I'm thankful
W-O-O-O-W
To be a child of THINE!

Bless You for what has been written
Before my time and placed in the Bible for my learning
It makes me want to keep running on
And for You and Heaven to keep yearning.

(Refrain): Uhm-m-m FATHER W-O-O-O-W!
I thank You
I bless You
LO-O-R-RD, I'm thankful
For the privilege of prayer
Uhm-m-m, I'm thankful
W-O-O-O-W
To be a child of THINE!

Rom. 15:4

TABLE OF CONTENTS

Look for the
Let Your Gifts Shine Forth Workbook
to journal your own faith journey.

Available on Amazon, from the author,
and from most major booksellers by request.

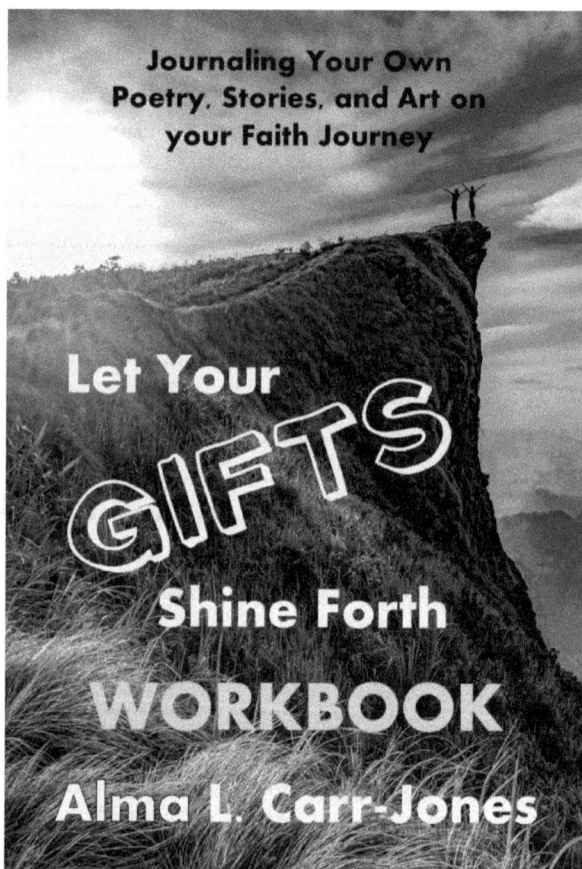

PREFACE

This book, originally entitled *W.O.W. created w.o.w.*, was a labor of love for me, love for you, and love of the LORD. I just had to share the wonders of His love with you as I am so excited about this book! And I am joyous about it as well because it is my attempt to tell the LORD how much I love Him and that I would stand on top of the tallest mountain in the world and proclaim my love! Let me see if I can share that love, excitement, and joy with you.

But first, let me lay a little groundwork. Because GOD wowed me, a sense of praise has been kindled within me as well as senses of obligation, gratitude, and of awe. The way to express my praise – and the way you can express your own praise – is to *Let Your Gifts Shine Forth*, so that others may see and know.

Why do I say that my FATHER has awed me to the point of wow? Okay, listen and I'll tell you. He has awed me to the point of my being made to realize that I am His creation and that, though I am but "pottery," He uses me for His purposes, according to whatever plans He has for me. Alright, let me take you further.

I know you remember the story of Moses in the Bible. (If you don't, then please do read it, beginning in the book of Exodus. You'll find that it makes interesting reading.) When Moses was tending the flock, (yes, a shepherd at this point in his life) GOD got his attention by showing him something so spectacular that Moses had to draw "near to see that riveting sight!" GOD awed him by creating a wonder to get his attention, a bush that would not burn up! We know how that story ends up, don't we? (Exodus 3:1-22)

Let me continue to run down the list of how my FATHER worked wonders that have awed me:

Further Biblical Days:

Daniel – He shut the lions' mouths and would not allow the hungry lions to eat Daniel! I can't even imagine keeping a hungry lion from his food, can you? (Just remember back when you were a kid and your dog (if you had one) wanted a bone very badly and you tried to keep it from him. My point exactly! (Daniel 6:1-24)

Hebrew Boys – He made a roaring fire forget how to burn! (Daniel 3:21-28) Yep, that got me too.

Water Congealed – He made a dry corridor through the midst of the sea for the Israelites to cross over. (Exodus 14:1-30) On this one, my eyes would have been as big as saucers, and you know what else? You know it; I would have been peeking through the wall of water as I ran and would have, at least touched the water wall once, unless specifically instructed not to.

Now-a-days:

A Tumultuous Thundering Waterfall – He made the waterfall that sends thousands of gallons of water over the edge, and it never dries up. Yes, that wows me! Where does all of the water come from? If I could travel the course of a waterfall as a water molecule, I would see if there is a circuitous route, however long, that made its way from A to Z and then back to A again. That, my friend, is something to imagine. And the GOD that we call Father orchestrated it all!

A Tsunami – He can roll the waters back away from the seashore so that people could, if they had a mind to, scoop up fish from the ocean floor with their bare hands! You know how you pull a string and the vertical blinds or the Levolor blinds slide smoothly back, well He has machinated this thing so well that water molecules go where He sends them and stay where He puts them. And I get to serve Him! Little *ole* me! Yes, I'm wowed!

Hummingbirds – He makes their wings beat an average of 53 beats per second (so fast that you can scarce see the wings). If you have never seen a hummingbird hover, then you are missing a treat. It seems as if they are standing on the wing of the air and He made it all and let me see the wonder in it. It's like He said, You like that? Well, here's what you do. You mix up this solution of sugar and water and add a little red coloring, put it out and you can watch the little fellows whenever you want to." *Somebody* might say, "Well, nothing so great about that. All you have to do is…" I beg to differ. The entire hummingbird scenario is riddled with awe, from the bird itself, to the sugarcane, to the simple genius of knowing how to build the feeder so that the bird's tongue can go into the "nectar", but the liquid, contrary to what we might think, hangs in the hot sun day in and day out and does not get too hot to touch; does not evaporate and does not seep out. The very first person to make a hummingbird feeder was not born knowing how. How did he grow from being a baby, who knew nothing when he came into this world, into a hummingbird feeder maker? Who built the brain that thought that up? The brain that absorbs info, turns it over and over and gets ideas of genius. Who is the ARCHITECT that constructed such a being of clay and had it walking, talking, thinking, etc.? Who did that? My FATHER did, that's Who! Yes, I'm wowed!

Thunder – He makes the thunder boom as well as the resulting tremor of the earth. You know when that thunder booms so loudly that you feel it under your feet and you think something like, "Yep there is a GOD and He is busy today. I'm glad that He loves me! I wouldn't want to make Him angry! Whew! That was a big one!"

Fall Foliage – He makes the reds, oranges, maroons, gold, etc. appear, thereby, wowing me with the splendor plastered across the landscape. Ever been wowed to the point that your breath was taken away for a heartbeat or so? If you have, then you know what I mean, and if you haven't, take the time to try it. You will wonder why you never noticed the beauty before.

The Rainbow – He placed one so that I could drive my car to it, pause while in the middle of it and look back at its beginning after I had passed completely through it. It was a magical experience and not one that I am likely ever to forget.

The Bible – the thoughtful planning and consideration that He inspired men to put therein wows me. It is the instruction manual that goes along with the "clay pot" that has been wound up and had a life blown into it. And we sometimes forget to read the instructions.

Love – the phenomenal gift of love through His Son wows me. You know how we don't want anyone bothering our children? Well, He allowed His only son to die for the likes of me. The way He brings me out of my troubles and sees me through my trials awes and amazes me, because as unworthy as I am, He still loves me and is faithful towards me. The endless love that He has demonstrated countless ways in my life amazes me. I don't really understand it, but I understand Him enough to know that He is faithful and that I owe Him. If I lived a thousand lifetimes, I could not repay Him, but I can pay on the debt. Know what I mean?

I could go on and on, but you, by now, know what I am saying. Folks, when I think about the fact that the BEING who put all-l-l of this together is mindful of me, I bow in obeisance. When I think that HE, not only is mindful of me but sends me joys, great and small, just because He wants to see me smile, I am awed. When I think about the fact that "I am a citizen of the United States and can't get a quick audience with the President any time I want, but can present myself before my FATHER's throne at any hour, day or night," I am awed and humbled.

I have told you a little bit about my journey. One of my gifts is writing, and this book is my way of saying to my LORD, "Thanks for my journey." Lastly, as I go forth to pen other tomes, I must admit that this particular book has burst forth from me. It made me introspective, which has been a profoundly, heart touchingly enlightening experience. This book has been like a "fire shut up in my bones" and I invite you to read with me through the stories, essays, and poems that I have penned for His glory as I endeavor to give Him praise and tell my story. While I may not have achieved (though I hope I did) my hope of igniting a similar fire in you, I present forth my gifts jubilantly and joyously, knowing that for the GOD I serve, I am "Doing What I Can, While I Can!" Hallelujah!

INTRODUCTION

Poetry is not a popular read, but I want to change that. Have you ever read a poem and wondered what prompted the poet to pen those exact words? Ever wondered what they thought when they wrote certain poems?

Have you ever had pain so great that you felt like no one could understand and/or had ever been through something like you had just experienced?

Have you ever had a moment of joy so piercingly sweet that you felt that you could melt or had your eyes well up with tears? Well, this poet has had such moments. So, I decided to write poems that speak to your joy or your pain. I decided to tell you why I chose certain categories to include in my poetry book. You see, to write about trust, I have to know something about trust. To write about perseverance, I have to have gone through some things and have learned to hope when hope was, seemingly, lost.

Some of the poems in this book will bring you to tears. Others will make you erupt in laughter. Whatever your reasons may be for reading my book, you will be moved, and you will find yourself picking up *Let Your Gifts Shine Forth* often. It is my hope that it garners hope within your breast and reminds you of a HIGHER POWER! Whether this book helps you a little or a lot, please pass forward any blessings you receive from it.

Category 1:
Life Plan/Amazement

By the Grace of GOD

An Open Letter –

When I received the following statement via email, I choked up:

You, my dear, are a blessing and I am honored that you have been a part of my life for almost 47 years! That's close to half a century.

Love you,
Joyce

This email just goes to show you, doesn't it? GOD placed Joyce in my path at the beginning of my college days, to be my friend, as I began my solitary walk after having left the comfort of my Momma's house and to traipse along in life. In retrospect, I can say, "Thank You, LORD, for Joyce!" Little did I know that she would become the sister that I never had, but He did!

This book of mine is the culmination of the hopes and dreams of a Memphis school girl who, because her mother told her to, "Reached for the Stars" and dared to say, "I'm *gonna* be somebody one day." Walk, if you will, back down Memory Lane with me a bit…

As she sat in the Guidance Office of Manassas High School, taking in her scholarship letter, she couldn't help but pick up her Memory Book and read some of the autographs that had been written by her classmates. One autograph stood out more than the rest, the one that read, "May your joys be as deep as the ocean, your sorrows as light as its foam and may you always have the wind at your back."

She idly wondered if the ocean had any foam. But one thing for sure, she would walk these halls no more. This would be the last day.

Tomorrow they all would graduate downtown at Ellis Auditorium. She had a new dress that her church had bought for her because her Momma could not afford a new dress and all graduates had to wear white.

Three Months Later...

She was going to college! She was going away from home. Momma was traveling on the Trailways with her. Momma would check her in and then Momma was catching the bus back to Memphis. Soon, she would be on her own. Yes! *(That too, is a story for another day.)*

College Graduation, Marriage, Two Adopted Children and Thirty Years Later...

The email that she had received that morning had made her wax sentimental. She looked back over life and thought about the big part that JESUS had played in it.

She thought about how He had brought her through so many trials. She reflected upon how He had held her hand when her Momma had died twelve years ago. She had thought that she would not and could not make it. But, because of the love of JESUS, she had. She thought to herself:

GOD (my beginning)
Love (crafted in)
A Plan
Care Packages (to sustain)
Love (gathered back with)
GOD (my ending)!

She thought to herself, "If I hold to His hand, since He created me, He will sustain me and gather me back to Himself, all in His good time. She sat with her head bowed as she reflected upon the various "care packages" that she had been gifted with throughout her life. She reflected upon the pink and green suit from her high school club days *(a story for another day)*; she reflected upon her scholarship; she reflected upon her best friend from her freshman college year, Joyce, etc.

As she sat around and reminisced, she realized that she had been shown favor by the LORD. Then she wrote:

When I think about the favor that GOD has placed on my life, I can't help but marvel at the fact that the GOD, Who orchestrated the cosmos; the GOD that initiated this thing we know of as time and placed a limitation there on; the GOD that one day will usher in eternity; takes the patience and places His omnipotent eyes and ears on a tiny speck of dust called Alma, I am agog! 'What am I that Thou are mindful of me?'

As she continued her reflecting, she realized that she had come far from the starry-eyed teenager who went to college with one pair of regular shoes and one pair of Sunday shoes and one dress skirt. As she finished checking her email, she finished up her reverie with a perusal of the news feed on Facebook. What she saw there, caused her eyes to fill with tears that slowly cascaded down her cheeks. Several of her former students had posted on Facebook giving her an outstanding *shout out* for her work while she was their teacher. She lifted tearful eyes toward the ceiling and said a grateful prayer to JESUS.

She realized that the starry-eyed teenager had had a successful teaching career in that she had made a positive enough impact on her students that some of them reached back and thanked her. She thought about the poetry books that she had authored and about this one that she was working on now.

She knew that all these positives in her life meant that JESUS, in His infinite care and wisdom, strategically wove the pattern of her life so that all things fell just so. Then she said, *"LORD, oh LORD! Can You hear me? It's me, Alma. And I just want to say Thank You!"*

Wind at My Back

The day that I left my hometown
To go off to school
Is a day that I'll always
Remember as being exciting and cool.

I left home with <u>stars in my eyes</u>
And the wind at my back
Courage came along with me to
Make up for the materials things that I lacked.

Didn't have any money to pay the necessary fees
And only had one pair of shoes
But I had hope in my soul, joy in my heart
And a FATHER to guide me.

I hit that dorm with a smile on my face
"Look out world; am here to begin my race
Don't look down on me
With your assumed superiority.

For you see before you a being
Who will take on any challenge
And whip this feat "lickety" split
Before you realize what you are seeing.

By the time you realize that
Here is a force to be reckoned with
You will discover that you have been bested
By the penniless one, without
Ever realizing that you were being tested!

Proverbs 8:32

What does the phrase, "stars in my eyes" mean from line 5?

What can you surmise from verse 4 about the speaker's personality? Self-concept?

Caring DEO

It is such a blessing to be loved by GOD
Because He gently guides you
Wherever your footsteps may trod.

Being a student of history,
Biblical and <u>secular</u>, both
Makes you see how
His omnipotent hands
Orchestrated(s) and
Detailed(s) the lives of man.

Psalm 119:133

What, in the poem, suggests that the LORD has a plan for our lives?

What does the word, "*secular*" in line 5 mean?

Expound upon how you think this poem fits into the Amazement
Section of this book.

Look

Look at what He has done
Through my poetry
He is bringing me to the place
Where He always intended me to be.

Proverbs 19:21

What is the speaker trying to say?

You Are Amazing

FATHER, You amaze me
The way You let me see
Some of the things You show me
In a moment of epiphany.

So I garner the things that You show me
And place them where You will
Using my parchment paper and
My new "voice regulated" quill.

Isaiah 50:4

Explain "*parchment paper.*" Explain "*voice regulated quill.*"

Literary Endeavors

Thank You for the book
And blessing me in all
Of the literary endeavors
That I undertook.

One thing about it
 When you decide to bless
There is no end to the
Intended recipient's success!

Isaiah 50:4

How do you know that the speaker thinks that the LORD is blessing
her/him in her/his literary efforts?

See You

See You in the gentle mist
That kisses the flower tops
See You in the morning dew
With its pristine water drops.

See You in the lava flow
That cascades down the mountain side
See You in the resulting obsidian
Found during the geologist's
Rock gathering pride.

See you in the torrent
Of the towering waterfall
That sprays a continuous mist
That settles on rocks, plants and all.

See You in the lightning strikes which
Spark fires to clean dense undergrowth
See You in the rolling thunder and the simultaneous
Tremor that causes the ground to pitch.

See You in the ocean waves
That crash the shore with its tide
See You in the invisible barriers
Wherewith, You make the waters subside.

See You in the stars that blink
Against the night sky
See You in the seasons as they
Continue to pass us by.

See You in the gentle breeze

That plays across my face
See You everywhere I look
As I continue to run my race.

See You so much in things beheld
See You through Your love for mankind when
You make sure that his life is going well.

Can't list all of the ways that
Your presence is seen and known
Just thank You, FATHER, for the knowledge
That I am loved and not alone.

And last, see You on the wings of the wind
When you take the fallen leaves
And make them swirl
See You in my mind's eye as You
Take Your majestic walk around Your world.

Psalm 104:3

Is the poet a student of nature? Substantiate form the poem.

What is meant by "*invisible barriers*" in line three of verse 5?

Expound upon the last line of the poem.

Outside My Window

I heard You outside my window this morning
But I didn't understand what You said
I heard You outside my window this morning
As from my morning meditation book, I read.

You spoke very loudly and it was easy to hear
For You boomed out some message that
Inspired in me, awe and fear.

I wanted so to understand the message in Your voice
But I could not fathom its meaning at all
But, as for listening, I did not have a choice.

I wished so that I could understand
What was being voiced as the thunder boomed
But, I am so glad that I can hear/feel the
Love that comes with such power
So I send my thanks to You, FATHER
For Your continuous care, in this stormy, predawn hour.

Job 37:2
Job 37:5

Is the poetess saying that the LORD talks to us?

Is Job 37:2 a fitting Scripture for this poem? Why?

Give another Scripture that can serve this poem as well. Explain your choice.

Water, Water

Water, water, water, water cannot
Live without you because, of you
My body's make up is 70%
Water, water, water, water
On a path through you
The <u>children</u> went.

Water, water, water, water
You keep us clean and you moisten our crops
For you are the essence of the tiny dew drops.

So beneficial in so many ways
Yet not to be taken for granted
Because you can become destructive
Whenever the need arises and
Wreak much havoc in the lives of man.

Water, water, water, water
A powerful element you may be
Makes one proud that you have a CONTROLLER
Who cares for all humanity.

Gen. 9:11

Find another Scripture for this poem.

Who are the "*children*" referred to in the last line of verse 1?

Concerning W.O.W.

W.O.W. is just the beginning of
Describing the GOD that I know
But when I pass "wow" in my <u>vernacular</u>
There is no place else to go!

So I go to His book
To get a formal description
I see omnipotent and amazing
When I do take a look.

While these words do indeed begin
To describe the GOD that I love and know
They leave me yearning to get closer to Him
And to that celestial city to go.

Gen. 8:22
Gen. 1:14

What does "*vernacular*" mean?

Build a Biblical paragraph around "vernacular."

Which of the two scriptures given, better goes with the poem? Why?

Alma L. Carr-Jones

Like a Moth to a Flame

You've drawn me like
A moth is drawn to a flame
And now I work, breathe and live
To bring glory to Your name.

And because I have this all
Encompassing love for You
I'll go; I'll be and I'll do
Whatever You want me to.

I will go and I will work and I will do
As long as my going, working and doing
 Bring ultimate glory to You.

You see, FATHER, I learned
 A long time ago that it
Is not all about me and what I know
It's about pleasing You and being
Committed to do Your will
It's about working in Your vineyard and
Staying faithful, while on the battlefield.
 .

And so, saying to my fellowman
"Make no mistake about it friend
I'm not out here to play
I'm out here to do my FATHER's will
As I wait on the foretold Judgement Day.

So, I will keep struggling on anyhow
Through the tears and through the pain
And through the sweat that sometimes
Coagulates on my brow.

Jeremiah 31:3
1 Corinthians 2:14

What does the world "*battlefield*" have reference to?

Planned?

My momma told me, a long time ago
That something bad been trying to
Get my attention all of my life
While I don't understand some of the
Weird happenings that I have been privy to
I do believe that everything will be explained
To me when due.

So I have to walk with patience on
And always try to do my best
For I do believe with all my heart
That my life was planned from the start.

Planned for what, I do not know
That has not been expressed to me yet
But the end result will not be average
On that I'm pretty sure that I can bet!

Jer. 29:11

Has the speaker had an average life?

What in the poem made you say what you did in your answer to #1?

Season to Season

Rain drops falling down
Leaves cascading to the ground
Ferns still with upraised arms
Lifted toward the sky
As the autumn leaves say hello when on
The wings of the wind, they pass by.

We had received an extraordinary amount of rain
For the year in McKenzie, Tennessee
The abundance of which made my potted plants grow
So fast that I could almost see
The tiny shoots unfold and the effect
On the petunias and snake plants was
Something wondrous to behold.

The plant that I thought was dead
From my home's gas winter heat
Took on new life and grew in profuse proportions under
The unusual amount of rain
Which was astonishing within itself
For I never thought that that plant would see life again.

A month later, while I still had an overwhelming
Sense of awe of the plentiful misty rain
My hummingbird friends decided to visit my patio again.

There were four of them this year
And one with a coral red throat
And I got the awesome chance to see them
Doing pirouettes and figure eights in the air
Ah-h, they make their mid-air calisthenics look so easy
And they do it with such a flair!

I had never seen that number of hummingbirds at one time
Let alone, seeing them right by my patio door
They sat around the feeder on the tiny wire support
That we had constructed
Then at brief intervals, their feeding
Ritual was conducted.

As I observed their antics, it looked to me
Like one was trying to chase two of the others away
While the fourth one seemed, not interested, at all, in the fray.

If I could have communicated with them, I would have, in a
Stern voice said, "Now, now, fellows, there is no need
To flap and buzz about
I have more nectar where that came from and
I will not allow the feeder to run out!"

Hummingbirds flying through the drizzle
Between the occasional downpour
To see those tiny-winged little fellows as part
Of GOD's natural system, I can't ask for much more.

My FATHER let me see the flowers and how they grew up
And He let me see the antics of the hummingbirds
As from the hummingbird feeder, they playfully supped.

My, my, the gentle loving care that was
Shown to me through the hummingbirds, and
Through the prolific flower growth
Reminds me of my FATHER's gentle nudging love
In that He made me aware of both!

I saw the spring rains and
Experienced the plentiful summer showers
I saw the return of the hummingbirds
And I saw the prolific growth of the summer flowers.

And now, I see the advent of another season
And the preparation as well as the
Migration that goes with it
Some animals are preparing to travel
To warmer shores
And some animals are storing up nuts and what-have-you
Against the time when nuts and berries will be few.

Some flowers have begun to put on seed pods
As <u>progenitors</u> of next year's flower crop
Plants and animals alike, getting ready for the next season
It makes me think of mankind's life span
And the fact that we too, need to make preparations fellowman
For our passage through time on our way to eternity
To be assured that the wailing and teeth-gnashing won't
Be coming from us, for we will be safe in our celestial abode
Where from tears and pain, we will, at last be free.

Gen. 8:22; 2 Corinthians 5:10

How does the speaker feel about spring?

Expound upon the term "*progenitors*" in a biblical sense.

Category 2:
Perseverance

You Can Do It

"Smoke! Somebody smells like smoke. Yuck!"

"One day, my clothes won't smell like smoke and one day…" Alicia thought to herself, then she went into her favorite pastime for when she was bored. She daydreamed!

"Alicia! Alicia Nicole Brown! Name the different types of prepositional phrases and give the class an example of one in a sentence."

"Uh-oh," she thought, as she snapped from daydream back to reality. "I only glanced over that page!"

She looked at Hank Gould, who had his usual "ready to laugh at you smirk" pasted on his face.

"I'll show him. Please make me remember what was on that page," she muttered to herself.

Alicia looked out of the corner of her eyes toward the ceiling and began to tell the types of prepositional phrases there were, as the page she had scanned slowly came into view in her mind's eye. She gave a sentence with a gerund phrase, looked at Hank Gould with a "Not today, you don't laugh at me," smile and triumphantly flopped back down into her seat.

"Nicely done, Ms. Brown, but try to keep up with the class. You might not get lucky next time."

"Yes Ma'am." She stole a look at Hank Gould and stuck her tongue out at him. He looked at Alicia with a "mess with me look" and blurted out, "Ms. Felicity, smells like something is burning and it's hurting my nose." Hank gave Alicia his best, "Now top that one, Girlie" glares.

The other kids chimed in, "Yeah, it does. I smelled it when I was passing out papers." "Yeah, it's been smelling like that all week."

Alicia dropped her head as her eyes slowly welled up with tears.

"That's enough class," said Ms. Felicity sternly. "It is probably a ballast in the lights going bad."

She glanced at Ms. Felicity and gave her a tremulous smile of thanks.

When the bell rang for class to be over, Hank walked by Alicia snickering, and whispered, "Cry baby!" as he left the room.

Sniff! Sniff! Alicia trudged slowly home. She could not walk slow long though, because the wind was cutting her in two! She put her arm load of books down on the sidewalk and buttoned her coat and put her head scarf on. Then she picked up her books, wiped her eyes and running nose on her sleeve, and kept pushing against the wind on her way home.

As she walked, she thought about what had happened in the last period class. "Maybe they will have forgotten about it by tomorrow." But with Hank Gould around, she knew not to count on it.

"One day, I'm going to be somebody; see if I don't," she muttered to herself. Alicia was so cold that she wished that some of the cars passing by would stop and offer her a ride. She did not mind the three mile walk on most days, but during the winter, it was rough.

She settled into her walking routine being sure not to step on the loose pebbles on the sidewalk because she had learned early on those loose pebbles hurt quite a bit when your feet are nearly numb with cold.

Alicia quickened her step. She would be glad to get home out of the wind. Whew, it was cold!

She had to pass a local consumer store every day on her way home, and when she passed it today, she saw a mound of shoe boxes piled up next to the dumpster. Alicia crossed the street and started going through the mound of shoebox trash. Lucky day! She even found a shopping bag with two handles almost intact. She left that dumpster with a hefty shopping bag full of smashed shoeboxes, their tops, and the accompanying tissue paper inserts. She wished that her brothers had been with her; then they could have brought all the boxes home. Alicia sighed and was thankful to have been able to get the ones she did.

(Rip-p-p!) The loose handle on the shopping bag ripped just as Alicia has started across her front yard. She tried to juggle books, boxes, and her pocketbook. She lost the battle with all three. Alicia was only a little bit embarrassed to have dropped her boxes. "So what if they see the empty boxes? They could be for a school project couldn't they?"

But Alicia knew she was not fooling anyone. She knew that everybody knew that their lights were turned off, in fact, probably had been peeping out of the window when the MLGW truck pulled the electric meters and turned the water off at the curb. They always made so much noise when they turned off the water. It was almost like they enjoyed clanking that long metal thing against the water cover like it was a gong. "Boy, they must really enjoy their job," was what Alicia had thought on more than one occasion.

She was glad to get into the house out of the wind. She was also glad to rid her aching arms of her cumbersome burden. She looked at the little gas stove in the living room and wished she could will it to come on. "Your daydreams are not going to get this charcoal bucket going," she thought.

Now that she had the charcoal bucket lit, Alicia reached over to put the rice in the small sauce pan that Momma had named "the rice pot." Well, wouldn't you know it; the water canister was empty. Leave it to her brothers, drat them! Well, nothing to do but get the canisters and get down to Auntie Bessie's house before it got dark and get some water. Back out into the wind she went. The walk to her aunt's house was about a block long on one street and about a half a block long on the other street. "I'm going to be somebody one day; see if I don't," she thought. "See if I don't!"

She hoped her cousins wouldn't give her a hard time about the water. She knew that her aunt had started dropping hints about how high her water bill had been being. She made it to her aunt's and knocked on the door, "Who is it?" her favorite cousin called from within.

"It's me," piped Alicia.

"Doors open; come on in."

Alicia went inside and started her routine of filling up the two canisters.

"Don't you ever get embarrassed about hauling that water? I wouldn't do it. That's what your brothers ought to be doing!"

"I know that's what my brothers ought to be doing," said Alicia. "But it's hard for Momma to make them do anything. You know they're teenagers and she can't make them do what she wants them to do and sometimes they make her cry. Somebody's *gotta* help Momma. So, I do it. I don't want to see her cry. Sometimes I hear her crying at night, and I don't like to hear Momma cry. So you know; I go get the water. It's okay. Now, about people laughing at me, they *gotta* laugh at something. If they didn't laugh at me, then they would be laughing at somebody else. Anyway, one day I'm *gonna* be somebody!"

Alicia hoped she didn't meet any of her friends on the way home because you could hear the water splashing against the sides of the canisters. Alicia's coat was wet on one side by the time she got back home because one of the canisters had developed a slow leak. She hung the coat up on the back of the door in the bedroom and closed the door. She hoped it would be dry tomorrow because that was the only coat she had. It was so cold in the bedroom that maybe her coat would not be dry, but she had to take the chance and leave it in the bedroom with the door closed because she didn't want to smell like smoke when she went to school the next day.

Alicia couldn't worry about Hank Gould nor anybody else, right then. She had to cook. She knew it would do no good to worry about him.

Alicia went back in the front room and put the rice on in the rice pot. While she rinsed the chicken with a cup of water. When the rice got done, Alicia set the rice on her makeshift table, the metal chair that was beside the charcoal bucket.

Since there was no flour, she battered the chicken in meal and then put the frying pan on with a small amount of lard to cook the chicken in. Alicia remembered to use a very small amount of lard because she knew that the lard had to last for three or four weeks.

Momma had taught Alicia how to stretch the lard. She knew to use the fatback grease for cooking cornbread. And she knew to put the fatback grease back in the grease can after she finished frying anything. She browned the chicken on both sides and then poured the extra grease into the grease can. She then put one glass of water and one fourth of an onion in the frying pan to let the chicken simmer. Alicia had to be careful that the water from the frying pan did not boil over onto the charcoal and put the fire out. She knew if the charcoal got wet, the room would get colder than it already was.

Then Alicia put more charcoal onto the charcoal bucket to warm the room a bit more.

Alicia got sick to her stomach because of the fumes from the just started charcoal. She had to go to the door to stick her head out to get fresh air so that she wouldn't be sick.

She always kept a headache in the evenings because of the fumes from the charcoal bucket.

After she had finished cooking, Alicia, again thought about her harrowing day at school. "But, that's alright. That's okay," she thought. "One day, I'm going to be somebody and I'm going to have pretty clothes and ain't nobody going to laugh at me then!"

*****

Many of those high school days and nights long after her mother had fallen asleep, Alicia would go to sleep herself, with her mother's words resounding in her brain and her prayers to JESUS on her lips. "Reach for the stars; I'm going to be somebody someday! Please help me to do it JESUS, please help me. *(zz-z-z-z)*

And she did just what she said she was going to do. She was a good student; stayed in school; graduated from high school with a small scholarship to college and went on to become a successful teacher.

Note: The only charcoal buckets in her life now are one of the numerous grills she owns. Alicia's life story says that if you persevere with GOD on your side, all things are possible. Romans 8:28 says, "All things work together for good for those that love the LORD" and Alicia Cothran is a prime example of that…

I hope you enjoyed the story dealing with perseverance and I hope that you enjoy the poems that are in this section of the book, as I have given you a chapter from Alicia Cothran's life, during a time when she had to persevere. I further hope that this book touches an answering cord in you and resonates to you, the fact that prayer to JESUS changes things if you only persevere.

Intro to Poem, "It's a Wrap"

Perseverance and prayer pay off. You know that? When you keep your faith and continue to persevere, it is so sweet when you get one of those tailor-made blessings that has your name written all over it! Tailor - made blessings come in all sizes, big and small. But I'm just so grateful for reminders that the LORD is mindful of me. It makes me feel so special, like I'm one in a million!

It's a Wrap...

A tiny pebble was tossed into a dry season riverbed
As it lay there unmoving day by day
The rainy season returned with its plenteous deluge
And the headwaters of the river grew as with raindrops
Aplenty it was fed.

The headwaters became a rushing mighty torrent
And swept all on its path toward the river's mouth
To meet the ocean's mighty current.

The pebble had been worn smooth
 By the mighty headwater's toss
And came forth a polished stone with a gloss
To travel with the ocean, the whole world around
Until such time as it was deposited upon a distant shore
And by a collector, at last, was found.

It was taken home and put among the finder's rare baubles
That had been discovered of old
Well, wouldn't you know it, that shiny pebble
Turned out to be genuine gold.

So let's remember to keep our heads up, no matter what comes up in our lives. He sees and He knows… Remember. "All things work together for good, for those that love the LORD." Rom. 8:28

Perseverance

I saw my Momma's faith
As I was growing up
I saw my Momma's tears
As she drank from the <u>bitter cup</u>.

I learned from watching her, the art of perseverance
And being resilient through my pain
I learned to love the LORD
And to His cause, true to remain.

1 Peter 4:13-16

What other section is this book could this poem be in and why?

Make pro and con applications to your life and the life of someone you know with reference to this poem.

What is meant by the term "*bitter cup*" in this poem?

Explain how the given Scripture applies to the poem

What can be surmised about the poet's view of life and faith?

Appreciate

That I am an average person is not
Something you can look at and decide
Because I have been in the lion's den
Made my trek through the fiery furnace
And have been tossed by life's swelling tide.

Come on; sit a spell and I will relate to you
How I made it over and how the
GOD of Heaven brought me through.

Just let me tell you about being between
A rock and a hard place
Let me tell you about some of the heartaches
That I have had to face.

Oh, you don't have time to talk
You have to go to a meeting in town
Sure I understand that you are busy
But please, take a minute and do sit down
Because the time may come when you need
To talk and I may not be around.

I want you to know the road I've traveled
I want you to know where I have been
In case you get into hot water one day
And need some tried and true problem solving
Counsel from a well-meaning friend.

…In short, you cannot appreciate my glory
If you don't know the hills
And mountains that make up my story.

2 Corinthians 5:20

What "sense of" do you get from the poem?

Does the speaker seem to have prior knowledge of an impending event?

What do you think is the relationship between the speaker and the person spoken to? Substantiate your answer.

Forgotten My Name

Joy has forgotten my name
And peace has lost my address
I feel lost and bereft, folks
I must confess.

Nevertheless, I keep putting one foot
In front of the other
As I make my way homeward
In hopes of seeing missed loved ones
And yes, most of all, my dear mother.

Yet, a resounding voice says to me, "Not yet
There are other tasks set for you
The goals of which you have not met."

"Just keep your faith and don't waiver
In your zeal to do as bidden for me
And remember, I am by your side
And, know that I love you and
Be assured that you have not lost favor."

Hebrews 4:15-16

What is meant by the title of this poem?

According to the 2nd verse, is the speaker hoping to make a trip soon?
To where?

What level of faith does the speaker seem to have? Quote from the
poem to substantiate your answer.

GOD Specializes

When you come to the river that seems
To be *uncrossable* and you pray and you pray
And it seems there is no hope for you
You ever think that GOD is saying, "No
You stay on this side of the river
I have other work for you to do"
Did you ever stop to think that He is saying
"Don't worry about the mountain and
The valley that you go through
Just remember that I am GOD
And that I have plans for you."

Jeremiah 29:11

How does the Scripture given for this poem correlate with it or does it?

Explain the title in three lines or more.

Gamut

You can run through the <u>gamut</u> of your emotions in a given day
But you always need to remember to hold on
To JESUS, Who, always makes a way.

You cannot put Him on your frame of time
You have to remember that He is the LORD
And He works things out according to
Whatever is on His mind.

Romans 8:28

Expound upon the word, "*gamut*" in the context of this poem.

Do you see "wait" in this poem? Where?

Stepping into Wings

You lost your joys a long time ago
And the tears have started and you can't stem the flow
Learn to go on, no matter how hard it may seem
Keep putting one foot in front of the other
Knowing that things will get better
And keep your eyes and heart on your dream.

<u>Those simple joys that from you have flown</u>
He will give you wings to again, make them your own
Then you can soar with the best of them all
Because sweet JESUS won't let you fall.

Isaiah 40:31

Explain how Isaiah supports this poem.

What is meant by the first line in verse 2?

Dare

Dare to hope and dare to trust
Dare to throw all of your worries
Into the <u>dug well</u> of the just.

Dare to hope that the worries
Land at the bottom of a dried up well
Or if the well has water, that
The worries never learn to, a rope repel.

Lamentations 3:21

What is the literal and figurative meaning of the term, "dug well?"

Build a paragraph on the last line of the poem.

Touchdown

To feel like you can't take another disappointment
To be afraid to hope for fear of being
Trampled of having those hopes dashed
Is to live life on the fringes and not
Get past the place where your world once crashed.

So, go enjoy all of the hope and possibilities that
Are yours for the taking, if only to be scooped
Up in the wonderful world of imagination.

Disappointments come and disappointments go
But to walk in the misty light of maybe
 Has caused many a person to step out on chance
And later to be victorious and able to do
The end zone touchdown dance.

Philippians 1:12

Explain the last line in verse 2.

What emotion embodies the speaker?

Penurious

I believe that I can make it
Through this <u>penurious</u> spell of mine
That I will get job to catch up on
My bills and everything will be just fine.

Did not get a job
To <u>extricate</u> myself from this mess
Instead was led to be an <u>entrepreneur</u>
And have feathered and expanded my nest.

Gen. 39:2
Deut. 2:7

Define *penurious, extricate* and *entrepreneur*.

Correlate Gen. 39:2 and Deut. 2:7 to each other, then correlate them both to this poem.

Oh, Oh, Oh

Oh, oh, oh, my grandmother is gone
And now I am all alone
The enemy will try to do to me, what they can
But I have a powerful Savior
Who still occupies Heaven's throne.

If He wills, He can come to my aid
Because the man that can <u>box with GOD</u>
Has never been born nor made
Though men think that they can
Run over me, roughshod.

So, I will wait and I will see
What destiny has determined for me
For I, like Joseph, who his brothers withstood
Believe that because of my faith, JESUS
Will "Work things out for my good."

Gen. 39:2

What mood is paramount in this piece?

What connotation do you put on the phrase, *"Box with GOD"*?

What New Testament Scripture can be placed with this poem? Explain
your choice and how it fits.

Get Back Up

Have you ever felt that
You got hit the hardest
Whenever your life was going well
You had all your angles figured out
And you were making all kinds of strides
Then trouble reared its ugly head
And from the top of the ladder you fell?

Well, you'll just have to pick
Yourself up and dust yourself off
And start your climb again with
Your feet shod with the preparation
Of the gospel of peace and your
Head covered with the helmet of salvation.

In short, you need to equip yourself
With the whole armor of GOD
(Christian battle gear)
Which you can read about in
Ephesians chapter 6, verses 13-18
Then you can deal with whatever
The adversary puts on you
Without resorting to hating
And without giving in to fear.

Ephesians 6:13-18

Take this poem and break it down verse by verse, into one or two words per verse. Then build it back up using events of your own.

Define *adversary* within the context of this poem.

I Still Retain My Dream

Factory closing, job cutbacks and poor economy
I lost my job and I lost my home
And though a broken person, I may seem
I keep going because, folks, I still retain my dream.

I've had to feel some sandpaper days
When my living situation got pretty rough
But I remain resolute in my conviction
That situations come and situations go
So, I still retain my dream.

The myriad of things
That happen to us
Are meant to damage our
Determination, it seems
But I am determined and ever
Move forward, onward because of
A sliver of hope that
Has been placed within me
"That I am bound to see the fulfillment
Of the destiny of my dreams."

Isaiah 40:31
Psalm 27:14

What, in your life or in the life of someone you know, would you call
"*sandpaper days*"?

Has the speaker in this poem experienced a lessening of faith? Why or
why not?

How Much More?

Have been broken many times
Only to be mended again
Can barely see how it all started
And cannot see the end.

One just has to keep plodding along
In hopes of a better deal
Realizing it matters not how much one hurts
Nor how tired one might feel.

Perhaps, life works much like muscles do
They get stronger only after they get sore
Yet, a body wonders what else life has in mind
One often wonders, "How much more?"

Hebrews 6:15
Matt. 11:27-29

Compare and contrast the faith of the speaker to that of the Biblical character, Job.

Name several things that the speaker might be referring to in lines one and two.

Gridlock

Locked in grinding wheels
That continue to turn
No matter how one feels.

Caught in a grip that is strong
Soaring above the gathered throng
Repeated dashes to the ground
Can a whimsy of hope still be found?

Still, hope thrives in spite of the tears
Through the twisting turning of the wheel
Till the operator kicks in the safety clutch
To unlatch the kill switch of the sprocket gears.

Exodus 3:7

What is the *grip* mentioned in line 1 of verse 2?

What is meant by *gathered throng* in this poem?

Explain the last two lines of the poem.

You and Me

The only thing I know is that
I have put all trust in You
I am counting on You, JESUS
To always see me through.

Most of my life, or as far back
As I can remember
It's been You and me
Against the rest of the world
So, I will be resolute and valiant
And keep stepping on though
The enemy's darts, at me are hurled.

Have found that in some situations
I am as dumb as a box of rocks
Yet, like a well-programmed automaton
I keep stepping on, in
Spite of life's hard knocks!

For one day, can say with the saints of old
Hallelujah, been tried by the fire
And by the grace of GOD
Have come through as pure gold!

Psalm 35

Define *valiant, resolute, hurled* and *automaton.*

What does "As dumb as a box of rocks" refer to?

Expound upon the last line of the poem.

If My Enemies

If my enemies come again
At me, in <u>full attack mode</u>
I'll just shift my armor to
Be sure of its fit and
Keep waging war under the
<u>Christian battle code</u>.

Psalm 3:5-6

What is meant by "*full attack mode*"?

Explain "*Christian battle code*" with reference to this poem and to the given scripture.

Like the Pine

Sometimes, as Christians, we have to be like the pine
That stands alone on the side of the hill
We have to weather storms and bitter winds
Yet, we have to keep standing, still.

We have to keep standing when
The world says, "Child, I wouldn't take that!"
We have to remind ourselves and them
Of the love that the LORD showed for us
By allowing His Son to suffer at mankind's whim
He didn't have to allow His Son
To die on that cross
But, because of His love for us
He would not allow our souls to be lost.

James 1:12

Explain the title with reference to the given scripture.

The phrase, "*storms and bitter winds*" refer to what?

Great Gain

GODliness with contentment is great gain
It causes me to stick and stay
With my resolve to be CHRIST-like
As toward Heaven I make my way.

It is not easy to be content
But it is a lesson that has to be learned
However, its rewards are sweet, in that
I no longer have to, for fulfillment yearn.

Philippians 4:11

Write a three-paragraph essay on, *"fulfillment yearn."*

Define *fulfillment*.

To Linda, (a.k.a. Lena)

In our efforts to find our way
To <u>eternity past time</u>
We sometimes have to cry because
Of the hills we often climb.

But we keep our faith in GOD
Because He indeed <u>orders our steps</u>
We've learned to keep plodding on
As His will, we have learned to accept.

Psalm 119:133

Explain the underlined phrase in verse 1.

Explain the underlined phrase in verse two. *(**Note:** Use the given Scripture in both of your explanations.)*

Yard Sale

We had our long planned summer
Yard sale of necessity today
And most of the things we sold
We just about gave away.

I was fearful of having the sale
At first because I worried that we
Might not have anything that people
Would consider worth a fee.

I need not have worried; the sale
Went off without a hitch
And my husband, who is a natural talker
Sold stuff without fail.

When we counted our coins and
Deducted our expenses and our change kitty
I felt loved, welcomed and proud
That we had chosen McKenzie
As our new hometown city.

The "necessity yard sale" reminded me
Of two things that I need never to lay aside
One, because He said He would
GOD will always provide
Two, to find a bargain, people
Will travel far and wide.

Yes, I sold some things that
I would have like to have kept
But I count it a blessing to have had stuff
That people deemed worthy of buying

Because through their generosity, I
Received a reminder, to always keep on trying.

So when <u>fortune smiles on me again</u>
And I can go to yard sales as a hobby
I will look back on my "necessity sale"
And remember to put something extra
In the seller's change kitty.

Job 29:4

Explain the underlined phrase in verse 5.

Explain the underlined phrase in verse 7.

Tie "*When fortune smiles on me again*" to the given scripture.

That's My Problem

That's my problem now
I have given and given and given
Until there nothing left for me to give
And now I am forced on <u>Need Street</u> to have to live

Yet, I don't <u>begrudge</u> the things that
I have done to help other folks out
I just wish that somebody would think
"Fair play" and turn my fortunes about.

…Still, if it comes about and fortune smiles on me again
I will still be willing to help folks out
But with a limit, for I bear the scars of remembrance
Of my generous "giving" pains.

Uh-m-m, I changed my mind; if I could go back and alter events back in time
I would still help my fellowman because it's in my nature to be kind.

Job 42:12

Define *begrudge*.

Explain, "*Need Street*."

Does the speaker begrudge his past generosity?

Adverse Times

When you find yourself in <u>adverse</u> times
You must continue to pray read and work
And don't allow situations in life to cause
You, your Christian duty to shirk.

No matter what hills and valleys you
May be faced with on your <u>sojourn</u>
Remember that your days are numbered
Just as sure as you were born.

We are all on a trip traveling toward eternity
And we know that we will be able to make the trip
Because of our <u>PATERNITY</u>.

The GOD that we serve is faithful and
He tells us in 2 Timothy, verse 15
So we have to use the Bible, which
Is the Christian's, GOD given life plan
That is chock full of inspiration and comfort
Inspired by GOD, for the good of mortal man.

Psa. 40

Define *adverse, sojourn* and *paternity.*

What does line 7 seem to imply? Explain that implication as presented in this poem.

Thought

Thought that if I pleased You
My life would be free from suffering
But it seems the more devout I try to be
The more sediment the currents of tribulation bring.

Seems my lot to be bombarded with
Physical pain, financial set back and emotional duress
But I keep striving to make it home
Where the saved will be eternally blessed.

I sought solace by regimenting a routine
Of simple physical activity
But that simple relief has been taken away
Because of excruciating pain in my heel
I never before realized how rejuvenated
My usual practice of exercise made me feel.

Still, I take solace in reading my
Bible and speaking, through my soul, to You
But I fear that I will awaken one day to find
That has been taken from me too.

The belief that You have a plan for
My life is what keeps me pressing on
And I'll keep leaning on You and trusting You
To never leave me traveling alone.

Still, I'll wait on You for the rest of my life
If that is what I have to do
Because, dear
Father, it is my goal
To spend eternity with You.

Hebrews 6:15

Define *sediment, tribulation, bombarded, emotional duress, regimenting, excruciating* and *solace.*

Explain "*More sediments the currents of tribulation bring.*"

What seems to be the speaker's level of faith? His resolve? Cite information from the poem to substantiate your assumption.

Life Teaches Well

Life is a good teacher since it has taught me
That it is not about material gain
Because the loss of all the "stuff"
You acquire, will cause you nothing but pain.

So I have, at last, learned the lesson
That my mother preached so well
"What matters is doing your Christian duty
So you will be saved from the fiery pain of hell."

Ecclesiastes 5:10

Make an application of the title to the given scripture.

Give another Scripture that could suffice for this poem.

Onslaught

An <u>onslaught</u> from the Devil
We are told to expect it
But it hurts much worse
When it is a family member
Who has <u>defected</u>.

I guess that we should not
Be surprised at even that
Because what Job's wife did
Is a documented fact!

Still, sometimes the pressure and
The pain cause our shoulders to slump
But we have to keep pressing on while
We strive to get over the road bump
Of heartache, disappointment and woe
Yet, we should still carry the gospel
Everywhere we go.

And the bumps along the road
As we make our journey toward home
One day will seem rather small to us
Because all of our worries and all
Of our cares, will at last, be gone.

1 Peter 1:5

Define *onslaught, defected.*

Make an application of the title to the given scripture.

Love the LORD

I love the LORD with all of my heart and this
Is a fact that is true, though I sometimes forget to
Do all of the things that He wants me to do.

When things don't go as they ought
In spite of my doing my best
I just hold to His unchanging hand
And try to stay the course and pass the latest test.

Don't get me wrong; it's not easy by any means
But I have a goal to which I am <u>aspiring</u> and that
Means taking on challenges, no matter <u>which way life leans</u>.

You see, I'm going home one day
To be with my LORD
So the chance of missing Heaven and entering hell
Is not something I can afford.

Philippians 1:23

Define *aspiring*.

What does the phrase, "*which way life leans*" mean?

Worse Days

Worst days are behind us
Why are we allowing the worst of us
To control the best of us
Why do we dress up that that is dying
And ignore that that has the capacity to live
Forever in the land of no more crying?

Romans 6:23

Write an essay of at least three paragraphs explaining this poem and its relationship to the given scripture.

Momma and the Rent Man

Blam! Blam! Blam! "Momma, somebody is at the door!" Louise knew it was the rent man because he came every Sunday morning to collect the rent. She was worried because the rent man knocked like he was mad. In fact, he had left mad last Sunday when Momma did not have his $10 in rent money. Louise knew that Momma did not have the rent money today either. She wondered what he was going to say, what he was going to do.

"Is he going to fuss at Momma?" Louise wondered. "JESUS, please help my momma. She was crying last night *cause* I heard her," Louise prayed.

Momma opened the door and the rent man entered.

"Something smells good in here, Lula Mae!"

"Yes sir, I fried some chicken backs for my children this morning," said Momma.

"Well, you got my money this morning?"

"No sir, I don't."

"Lula Mae, I told you last week to have my money!"

"Yes sir, you did. Can you give me one more week; I can catch up on the rent, sir."

"What is going to be so different by next week that you can have my rent money?"

"Well, sir, I do day work and I got another day this week," said Momma.

"Day work pays by the day," he said. "If you got a new day this week, you ought to have my money this morning!"

"I did have it, sir, but they came to cut the lights, gas, and water off and I had to pay it to keep my children from being cold and in the dark, sir."

"You took my money and spent it. It is not my problem about your lights! I want my money, all of it by Sunday or I want my house! If you don't have my money Sunday, I will be bringing the police with me to set you out! You understand me, Lula Mae?" His voice boomed.

Momma cleared her throat and said, "I've always paid you on time. I have only missed these two weeks and that is because I lost all my days."

"Lula Mae, your explanations don't mean a freaking thing to me! They are just like when a dog farts. You got nothing but a bad odor. And if you got rid of some of these dogs you got around here, you might be able to pay your bills on time!"

"Now you listen here; you can't tell me what I can or cannot have in my house! These dogs belong to my children. And the dogs don't cost nothing, because unlike some folks we feed our dogs bones, Mr. Rent Man!"

"You know what, don't bother getting the rent; I want my house vacated by Sunday!"

"Now see here Mr. Rent Man, you can't…"

"Excuse me, good morning, Mr. Rent Man." Louise timidly approached the man.

"Uh, good morning, Lula's little kid." He stormed down the steps and out of the yard.

Momma closed the door and said, "Whew!"

Then she turned to Louise and her two brothers and said, "I want y'all to go down to Slugall's Grocery and get me some moving boxes after church today."

A general chorus of "Aw-w Momma, do we have to?" went up. Louise piped up and said, "I got to get my homework," because she knew what store Momma put in by her good grades.

"No argument!" Momma yelled with tears swimming in her eyes. "Okay?"

"Okay Momma," said Louise and her two brothers.

"Come on sit down on your bucket so I can comb your hair for church," said Momma.

Louise thought to herself. "I prayed to JESUS to help Momma and I know He saw her crying last night…"

Louise ran to get the lard can that she used as a stool for when Momma was combing her hair. For once, she did not argue back, nor grumble at all, not even when Momma yanked the knot too hard in the kitchen area (the back part of the head). Louise was preoccupied.

She couldn't wait to get to church because she had to talk to JESUS.

In Church

Hey, JESUS, It's me. You did not help Momma today and I thought that we were going to have to move. The rent man, Mr. Smith, got mad at Momma and he was yelling at her, and Momma kept saying sir to him. He kept yelling and Momma started yelling too! He told Momma that we have to move and now we have to get boxes from Sluggall's after church today. JESUS, I don't want to move. I like this neighborhood and some of the neighborhoods here in Memphis are not safe. They have people that will beat you up. Some of the neighborhoods we don't even walk through because the people are so bad. I know we don't have hot water in this house, and I know that we don't have good heat. And I know that the kitchen stove smokes up everything so badly that all the curtains and the walls are black.

But JESUS, this is home and I'd like to stay here for long time. Will you help us JESUS? I know that you can because every time I cry and talk to you and sometimes when I get worried on the inside, you fix it. I want you to fix this too, JESUS, because I don't know what to do. I'm only a little girl. I wish that I could get a job, then I could help Momma. She had tears in her eyes again this morning, JESUS, and I don't like to see my momma cry. It makes me want to cry too. Please help our momma. Thank you, JESUS. Amen.

Louise was quiet all through service. She didn't even look around to see who was talking or passing notes. She listened to the preacher, and she didn't even get sleepy.

She was thinking about JESUS and about how she could help her momma.

When church was over Louise went to see the next-door neighbor, Mrs. Fanniebell.

She liked Mrs. Fanniebell because she gave Louise $0.50 every Saturday to go to the store for her.

"Mrs. Fanniebell," she tried not to sound whiny, "will you give me the $0.50 for going to the store for you early?"

"Well, I don't know about that, Louise."

"But, Mrs. Fanniebell, if you don't, then we *gonna* have to move." Tears welled in Louise's eyes. "The Rent Man said …"

"Naw, don't tell me. I heard him yelling at your momma. I don't know what good this $.50 will do, but I'm going to give it to you because you are a good girl and I don't want to see you cry."

"Yes ma'am." Louise wiped her eyes. "Thank you!" She offered Mrs. Fanniebell a big grin in place of the tears.

When Louise got back home, she was not surprised to hear Momma say, "No need to go and get boxes today; you can get them after school tomorrow."

Louise said, "Yes, Ma'am," with a smile in her voice and on her face.

Momma noticed. "What you smiling about?"

"Nothing, I was just thinking about church today."

"Now, Louise." Momma's voice was stern. "Don't go getting your hopes up; we have to move, and you get yourself home from school tomorrow and get the moving boxes from Sluggall's, you hear me?"

"Yes Ma'am." Louise lost some of her happiness because of Momma's words, but not all of it. She decided to keep the happy secret that she shared with JESUS to herself. She knew; she just knew that if she could talk to the Rent Man, he would not make them move. She just knew it; she didn't know how she knew it; but she knew.

The Next Day

School seemed so long the next day, but Louise did not care. She had something important to do when she got out. She stopped by Sluggall's on the way home from school and picked up the four moving boxes.

She asked Mr. Sluggall to let her use one of his grocery carts to haul her books and the boxes. He did. Louise got home; put the boxes down along with her books; grabbed her pocketbook and went back out. She was so glad that they had started the street bus to coming right in front of their house. All she had to do was walk about 500 feet to the corner and wait for the bus. She was in luck and did not have to wait long. After she found herself a seat on the bus, she watched the people as they got on and off the bus and wondered what their life was like. Then she grew tired of people watching and said another quick prayer to JESUS to add to the many times she had already prayed that day.

Okay, her stop was coming up. "Here goes; hop off," she thought. Louise's leg started shaking and her throat felt like her voice was going to come out scared and squeaky. Well she was! But she was not going to let the people inside the Cotton Exchange Building know that!

She walked up the steps, wiped her sweaty hands on her dress, and went inside the door. She saw a lady and asked her, in with her best schoolgirl voice, where Mr. Fred Smith's office was. She told the lady, "Momma sent me to pay the rent." She hoped the lady didn't say something like I'm his secretary; you can give it to me. The lady didn't and Louise was relieved because she didn't have any money to pay anybody. All she had were her prayers to JESUS, bus fare back home, and a dime to buy a stage plant cake with; that's all. She went in Mr. Smith's office and the door almost shut on her because she was so little, and the door was so heavy.

Mr. Smith looked up distractedly from his desk.

"What do you want little girl?"

"Excuse me, Mr. Smith. My name is Louise and I'm Lula Mae's daughter. We live on…"

"I know where you live and I know your Momma," he interrupted.

"Yes sir, well I used my $0.50 that I get for going to the store for Mrs. Fanniebell to come and ask you not to make us move. Momma cried when you left, and I don't like to see my momma cry." She fought her own tears with a sniffle. "It makes me want to cry too." She took a deep breath. "I can chop cotton to help Momma pay the rent. Will you please let us stay? I have ten cents left from the bus. I will give you that and Momma will only owe you $9.90."

Mr. Smith cleared his throat and gruffly handed Louise a tissue. He said, "Okay, put the dime on the table and tell Lula Mae I will see her on Sunday. You tell her I want $9.90!"

"Yes sir! Thank you, sir!"

Louise turned and put her dime on the table and left his office. Her legs flew down the steps. She skipped all the way out to the bus stop. She did not know, but just in case Mr. Smith was looking, she put the happy little girl step in her skipping. She knew that she was a good skipper and she knew that JESUS had come through for her again.

She thanked Him on the bus all the way home. She did not forget to pray to JESUS to let Momma not be mad at her and not to whip her. She wanted to get home before Momma did so she could cook and wash the dishes to put Momma in a good mood. No such luck! Momma was standing in the door. She didn't look mad, but she didn't look happy. Louise put on her best *Momma guess what* excited skip. She said, "Momma! Momma! He said we don't have to move! Momma, he was happy. And I was not scared to ride the bus down there."

Momma looked at Louise like she had two heads and purple hair. She found the chair by the door on the front porch and sat down with a *woof!* Louise, ever mindful of trying to keep from getting a whipping said, "Momma, Momma, are you alright? Do I need to get you some water? Huh, Momma, huh?"

"Yeah, bring Momma some water, Pooch."

Louise skipped into the house and got the water. She knew that Momma was not going to whip her. She figured she might get fussed at a little bit, but she didn't care. She had talked to JESUS, and He had answered her prayer!

When Louise handed Momma her water, Momma gave her a deadpan stare and said, "Okay, tell me how you got the money to go downtown."

"Well, Momma, after I prayed to JESUS, I thought, go ask the Rent Man not to make us move. And I got my money from Mrs. Fanniebell, and I used that." Seeing Momma's mouth twitch, Louise continued in her best storytelling voice like she had heard Momma use so many times. "And I wasn't even scared, but my leg was shaking a little bit." She recounted for Momma the entire episode, even down to her happy little girl step in the middle of her skipping. She and Momma laughed about that.

They sat quietly together for a few moments, then Louise broke the silence.

"Mommuh-h?"

"What?"

Sheepishly, Louise asked, "Prayer works don't it, Momma?"

"Yeah, I declare it does," said Momma, looking at Louise once again like she just saw her for the first time.

Later that night as she went to bed, Louise thanked JESUS for not letting her Momma whip her and she thanked Him most of all for making the Rent Man be nice and letting Momma keep the house. As she sleepily drifted off, Louise wondered what would have happened if she had asked GOD to make the Rent Man give her a job... *(z-z-z-z)*

Louise always remembered what Momma had told her about prayer and remains a faithful, prayerful Christian to this day, for she knows that *Prayer changes things*!

$35 A Week

$35 a week is not very much
That is what the lady lived on
And she took care of three kids, with such
Meager earnings at this –
Life in her household was anything but bliss.

But she drove her children forward
With the determination that was fierce
Reach for the stars was what she always said
As through the homework laden night
Her strident voice would often pierce.

Her relentless struggle for her children
And her stalwart belief in GOD
Gave that tired mother more than enough
Stamina to last, even when the tide was tough.

She got her children through school
And saw them become productive young adults
She got to bump her first grandbaby on her knee
And lived to see that he was the first in a long line
Of her blessed posterity.

At the close of her long life, she looked
At her daughter with a satisfied smile
And said, I am proud of your accomplishments, daughter
And I'm glad that you took a page of learning from me
But most of all, I am thankful that the GOD of Heaven
Sent you to be my child.

A tribute to Lula M. Carr, My Momma

Which do you think was written first, the poem, "$35 A Week or the story, "Momma and the Rent Man"? Why? Give evidence from the poem and from the story to substantiate your assertion.

In line 8, what does *Reach for the stars mean*?

Define *strident* from line 10.

Make a biblical application to the poem. A personal one.

What to Do, What to Do

You must not spend your time wringing your hands in despair
Instead, do yourself and your fellowman some good
And spend some time in prayer
You will find a faithful FATHER
Waiting for you there.

Hebrews 4:16

What is the mood of the poem?

Compose a short essay of encouragement to go along with the poem in answer to the title.

Category 3:

Prayer

That prayer gets results is a known fact
And since lifting up CHRIST is what we are all about
It's <u>tantamount</u> that we pray for growth
And that we pray for leaders and laymen both.

You pray for your families, sons, daughters, etc.
So, right behind that prayer for your family, as often as you do
Pray for the rest of the church (world-wide and local)
Because they need your prayers too!

Ephesians 6:18

Define *tantamount.*

What does Ephesians 6:18 say about prayer?

Listen to Me

Listen to me; I am telling you the truth
Talking to the aged, middle aged
And to <u>resilient</u> youth.

Make sure that your prayer life
Is in accord with His will
Because, whatever you ask
According to His will
Your needs, He will fulfill.

Philippians 2:14-15

Define *resilient*.

Make the application of the title to the given scripture.

He Came Down from Glory

He came down from glory
To write the end of mankind's story
He came to see about me before I was
Formed in my mother's womb
JESUS died for me.

I know that He will come to see about me now
If I just humbly approach His presence
And before GOD's throne I bow.

John 17:20

What is the mood of this poem?

What epitomizes the speaker's faith?

Tell how John 17:20 correlates with this poem?

In a Fix

If you find yourself in a fix
Though you have tried to do your best
Ask the LORD to help you and then
Take a much needed and deserved rest.

1 Peter 5:7

Find another Scripture to match the given text.

Showing Up and Showing Out

How does it feel to know that you prayed and caused GOD
 to show up and show out
It should make you feel special and very loved
It should make you want to tell everyone
What the GOD you serve is all about

Luke 11:13
Hebrews 11:16

Explain the title.

Which Scripture best coincides with what the title means. Explain.

Ladies' Day Speaker

Haven't spoken for a ladies'
Day in quite some time
Plus, it's the first time I've done
My speaking with a PowerPoint presentation
So to say that I am nervous
Does not begin to cover the situation.

I always try to bring my
"A" game when I speak
But I fear that tomorrow's lesson
As a speaker, will make me look weak.

Yet, I still have several hours
In which to try to bring out my best
Because when I speak about my FATHER
I don't want to make a mess.

"LORD, please help me get this lesson
Together in a cohesive fashion
 Please infuse my brain with your glory
And help me tell a heartfelt story."

...I needn't have bothered fretting
About my lesson for the day
Because my FATHER's love caused Him to
Send a plethora of inspirational thoughts my way.

James 1:6

Define cohesive, *infuse, heartfelt* and *plethora.*

Most of this poem is filled with what?

Who is the speaker talking to?

Apply James 1:6 to this poem.

Write a poem that epitomizes the given scripture.

Nestled

I came upon a little chapel
In the Smoky Mountains last fall
Man's inherent desire to worship is what
The presence of that little chapel made me recall.

Someone was thoughtful enough to
Be considerate of their fellowman
And erect a small place for prayer
For all who desire to worship, and in praise, to share.

Hebrews 10:25

Define inherent, chapel.

Is this poem aptly named? Why or why not?

Find another Scripture for this poem and tell why this Scripture fits the poem.

Comin' Back

The time is ripe for prayin'
There is no more time for playin'
Get ready; He is comin'
Back, is what I am sayin'.

Proverbs 3:5-7

Expound upon the given Scripture by explaining it and encapsulating
the essence of the poem within your expounding.

Select another fitting title for the poem and explain why it is fitting.

Ridicule

You found it worth ridicule
When I said in the sun in prayer
You found it worth ridicule
The length of time that I spent there

You found it worth the ridicule
When I kept my hands in thankful praise
But you did not find it funny at all
When I lifted my hands in prayer
In answer to your distress call...

Zephaniah 2:8-11
Luke 22:63-65

Is the speaker resentful of the person being spoken to? Substantial.

Compare and contrast any two of the given scriptures while elucidating the point referenced by the poem.

Nothing Else I "Ain't"

You think that you can tell me to pray
Whenever you see fit, but that will not
Work brother, for I pray a certain time each day.

You think that you can tell me not
To sing certain Zion songs
But that will not work brother because
I sing about whatever befalls my lot.

You think that you can tell me
Not to dress like a saint
But brother hear me when I say
"I am what I am and nothing else, I ain't!"

Col. 4:5

Tie the given Scripture in with the title.

Does the speaker seem to care what others think of her Christianity?
Substantiate.

Category 4:

Faith/Trust

Faith

I heard a preacher say, "Faith is not faith until it is put to the test!" *(I was to later, learn exactly what that meant!)* I had been a pretty faithful Christian all of my life and knew it too. At least, that's what I thought. Faith is defined as the *substance of things hoped for, the evidence of things not seen.* That's all well and good, but you know what I have discovered about faith? I have discovered that because you can't see it, it is hard to hold onto faith when things get rough in life. That proved to be so in my case, at least. But let me tell you a little bit about my faith and the journey we've been on together.

Second Chronicles 32: 31 says that Hezekiah was deliberately left alone as a test to see what he was really made of. GOD knows everything so this verse was pretty confusing to me at first. I mean how could GOD test Hezekiah to see what was in his heart when GOD already knew? Then I had a Minister to explain it to me that the LORD tests people, not so He will know what they will do, but for the strengthening of a person's faith.

Okay, that I could understand. Now, all I needed to figure out was, how long my test was going to last. But you know, it seems the more that I persevered and tried to remain faithful, the harder I got hit! Have you ever found yourself in such circumstances?

I was beginning to feel like Job of the Bible days. I mean, I knew that GOD saw my pain, my confusion, and my dwindling faith, so I knew that eventually He would make things let up. I knew He would if I just hung tough and persevered. So, I hung tough past my tired point, past my crying point, past my groaning point, past my mad point and up to my faith bothering and waning point. Through all these points, I continued to pray, though not as often and not as much. I knew that GOD used to love me and so, the only thing I could think was that He didn't care anymore. I reasoned within myself that, if things were happening like that to my child, I would step in and stop it quickly! Through all my times of trouble, I kept wondering where He was and why was He not helping me anymore.

Then I read the book of Job where the LORD told Satan to touch all that Job had, but not to lay a hand on him. Then I read that he was told that he could touch his body, but not kill him. THAT is what made me stop and do a double take! Then I started thinking, so that means that all of this *stuff* that I have been going through, the LORD not only sees, but He has the final say-so in all that happens in my life! That, dear reader, brought me a new word in my arsenal of faith, **ultimately**! The word "ultimately" is defined as *maximum, final or supreme*. That word said to me that when all has been said and all has been done, the buck stops here. That meant with the LORD! "Ultimately" carried me through my crying trying times **(C/T)** times or my trouble. This word, ultimately, allowed (and still does) me to look at my C/T times through the eyes of faith *(with rose tinted glasses)* on. Looking through those rose-tinted glasses of faith made my adverse situation look better. During some of my C/T times in my life, I have had to shed tears like I saw my Momma do when I was a little girl. These kinds of times will come at various points in all our lives.

So, dear reader, allow me to say to you, if you have problems that you have been worrying about and wrestling with, give it to GOD. Put it into the hands of SOMEBODY bigger than you and then let go. Give it to JESUS and let your faith work for you. So whether your C/T time is composed of sickness, financial trouble, bullies, etc. *Ultimately* says that your Goliath or your Pharaoh has met his match! Listen to this; if the LORD is for you, no matter what adverse situation you may find yourself in, you always do like cream and rise to the top! And what causes the cream to rise to the top? Why the churning of course!

If you and I will keep our faith when the ordinary person would lose it, that says something about us. It says like the Hebrew boys said Daniel

3:17-18, "If the LORD does not deliver us, it is not because He cannot and we still won't bow down." I paraphrased those two verses, but you understand it well enough, don't you?

 Let me give you another little scenario to help you see what I'm talking about. In the neighborhood where I grew up there were several large families. If you got caught without your big brother, then you might be in for a beat down from the neighborhood bullies. But then you go home and tell your big brother and he takes you back to the scene of the beat down and confronts the bully and takes care of business for you, making sure that the bully knows not to bother his little sister again.

The scenario that I just presented can be applied similarly to our Christian life. That is where ultimately comes in. You see JESUS is my big Brother and when I am confronted with stressful situations, calamities, enemies, etc., I take it to my big Brother. You might ask "How do you do that?" I do that through the avenue of prayer. As an aside, let me say that prayer must be a powerful tool! Why do I say that? I say that because enemies get bothered when a Christian starts to pray. Whatever you do, don't allow someone or something to break your faith in GOD because if they break your faith in GOD, then you won't pray. If you stop praying, you will stop talking to GOD and when you do that you will have lost the source of your help, your best friend!

So, I want you to get into the habit of talking to GOD. When you do, you will build that relationship of faith and trust that is so important to the LORD and is important to you, as well. You see if you get into the habit of talking to Him, you will look upon Him, as not only your FATHER, but as your friend, too. There is a song that says, "What a Friend We Have in JESUS" and truer words were never spoken.

So what to do in C/T times:

Keep going.

You do not give up.

You remember Who your FATHER is and exercise the spiritual privilege of prayer.

You remember that all is never lost, though the price of continued faith is often exorbitant! What you don't do is give up on your faith. You keep those rose-tinted glasses on.

Be mindful of the fact that if you give up on your faith, the next step is that you will give up on GOD. Then the adversary has you just where he wants you, at his mercy and he has none!

You read your Bible and call to mind the numerous times that the LORD has come to the aid of His children. You remember His track record by remembering Daniel, the Hebrew boys, and Joseph, to name a few.

You read the 46th chapter of the book of Psalms.

Whenever I'm going through C/T times in my life, I read that passage and then I talk to my JESUS. And this is the gist of what I say to Him:

Owing to Your faithfulness, JESUS, I know that everything in my life is going to be okay because You have already told me so in Your word. I have just finished reading the 38th chapter of the book of Job and Psalm 46. So for the times, as now, that I have a thought in my mind, "This isn't fair what's happening to me... But I didn't do anything..." I repent, JESUS, for I am so sorry and ask You to forgive me. You see, JESUS, I forgot to remember that ultimately, everything that happens in my life, You have control of. I also know that when Job was going through what he was going through, nothing could happen to him without Your say-so. You limited how much the adversary could do to him just like You limit how much turmoil the adversary can inflict upon me. I ask You to strengthen my weakening faith and help my unbelief.

In my concluding portion of this fireside chat, I want to tell you that there is a reason for everything that happens in your life. I have been allowed to learn that in my travels along this journey through time. Let me tell you what else I learned when I was allowed to experienced C/T times. I learned the true meaning of Romans 8:28. I learned that all things in my life are connected because they were planted in my path. I learned, even more, that my life is not all about me. I learned to look for blessings in my troubles (C/T times). I learned to be a blessing to someone else, even in the midst of my own storm. I learned to take whatever materials I landed upon and had to hand and prayerfully use them to the glory of the LORD! I learned that, "It is in the valleys that I grow."

I learned to tell people that I meet
It is not about you and me
It is about the ending of time
And the ushering in of eternity!

In short, I learned to lean fully on the LORD and to exercise an even deeper trust in Him, that I didn't even know was possible. I learned to shine my light, even when in the midst of the darkness of trouble, by exercising the wonderful special blessing called prayer. I learned in all of my circumstances to say, "To GOD be the glory!" I learned that my troubles draw me closer to Him who holds my life, your life and all of eternity in His hands. I learned that there are no problems that He cannot handle and is not aware of in my life.

I hope that I have given you encouragement if you are experiencing C/T times in your life. And remember to keep your head up, no matter what comes up in your life. He sees; He knows and *ain't* no surprises creeping up on Him. Allow me to leave you with these final words "Ultimately, JEHOVAH NISSI still occupies Heaven's throne and if you are His child He's got your back, so keep the faith!"

Compare and contrast JEHOVAH NISSI and JEHOVAH SHAMMAH in a two-paragraph essay.

Read About It: Find two other characters in the Bible where, because their faith was tantamount, GOD came through for them. Expound upon these two scenarios by telling what might have happened if these characters had done the opposite of what they did.

Life Application: give two positive examples of similar situations in your life, the outcomes and the lessons learned in each.

For His Glory: Prepare a 2 to 3-minute discourse for a non-Christian, using numbers 1, 2, or 3 above. This is done in a restaurant setting.

When Life Throws You a Curveball

… In tears, "Granny, why did he?" "Listen baby, when life
Throws you a curveball, sometimes it can be very hard
But you have to do what you have to do and
You have to reach your goal, yard by yard."

"You think you have all of the answers about
Everything that you're planning to do
But you just don't know, you have no idea
What fate has in store for you."

"Sometimes it can be so bad that you cannot
Figure out what to do in your situation
Sometimes you can be so down and out
You wonder about the reason for your creation."

"But then you remember that the GOD of Heaven
And all of His ominous power
Has sheltered and protected you
Minute by minute and hour by hour."

"Then you have to be resolute
And keep going on and on
You have to be able to see past the storm
To the sunny skies beyond."

"And it will always pay to remember
What my momma told me long ago
"Keep your faith in GOD baby
No matter the row that you have to hoe."

"And never forget to stay prayed up with your Bible well read
Because I have been living along time

And I have never gone unclothed nor unfed."

"Wait a minute baby
Just a few minutes more
GOD will take care of you
And about that there is no maybe!"

"He warmed me with the cloak of perseverance
When the cold winds of doubt and fear were raging
He dazzled me with His foot work
As He stepped into my battle fray
And always came out victorious
At the end of the day."

"One of these days, you will look back on this
And remember how He brought you through
And you will be able to talk to your children
When they come complaining about Him to you!"

Psalm 46

Define *resolute*.

Explain the meaning of the title.

What do think has happened at the beginning of the poem?

Does the speaker speak from experience? If so, give several instances from the poem. If not, give several references from the poem to support your conclusion.

What is the general theme of the poem?

Name a possible sub theme.

Plans for Me

When I think about the fact
That You have plans for me
It makes me want to run on
And be the best that I can be.

It makes me want to step high
And then step higher still
It makes me want to encourage others
To get to know You and to always do Your will.

When I think about the fact
That You have plans for me
I get a buoyancy in my step
That is easy for all to see.

And You know what; I don't care that they make
An example out of or make fun of me
Because I am striving to please You, JESUS
Whether through precipitous winds or calamity.

For I know to trust in You, no
Matter what comes my way
Because I know that about what
Happens to me, You have the final say!

Psalm 5:11-12

Define *buoyancy, precipitous*, and *calamity*.

Explain the application of this title by explaining the appropriateness of it.

Held

Held
Holds
Will hold
You in His arms
Where you were, are and will be
Safe from eternal harm.

Isaiah 41:10

What does tense have to do with this poem? Explain its usage.

Ever Stop to Think?

Do you know or ever stop to think about
Why the words of a song
Seem to play across your emotions
And stroke you from within and without?

Do you know or ever stop to think about
Why a verse from a poem or a famous
Quotation you have heard
Replays itself within your brain
Until you have memorized every word?

Do you know or ever stop to think about
The glory of the CREATOR
Spreading His love to you so that
You won't be undone by the <u>potholes</u>
And stormy trials that you are forced to go through
That these are just sweet reminders
That He cares much for you?

1 John 3:1-3

Define *potholes* both literally and figuratively.

Compose a poem that goes along with the given scripture. Use at least
two words of, at least, ten letters.

Sometimes You Get Tired

Sometimes you get tired
Sometimes you get worn
Sometimes you feel like you're walking
On your journey all forlorn.

Then faith takes a stand and reminds you
Of the road you've traveled so far
How you felt just as bereft back then
And yet, He brought you through.

So fellowman, pass that microphone
To faith a little more often
Then that bitter shell of <u>disillusionment</u> and weariness
Through faith's coaching, will begin to soften.

Matthew 11:27-29

Define *disillusionment.*

How could this poem have fit under the heading of Perseverance as well as this one?

Explain the last line of the poem.

Upon Swift Changes in Life

What is going to happen now
I have no idea
But I have learned to trust in GOD
And about trouble, not to worry nor fear.

Whatever swift changes are
Waiting for me down the road
I trust my JESUS to not let me
Be overwhelmed by the load.

Isaiah 40:7-8

Explain what is happening in the first verse.

After reading verse 2, you can surmise that what has happened?

Write an essay on Isaiah 40:7-8. Bring in one other Scripture to correlate or substantiate.

(*Senryu*) Strong?

I used to be strong
Though worn down to a frazzle
Faith pushes me on.

Romans 8:31-39

Define *senryu*.

Write a *senryu* dealing with the given scripture.

What is the status of the speaker's faith?

Where Do I Go?

Where do I go from here
Because life has taught me bravery
And death has taught me fear.

Never-the-less, I have learned to face
Each new challenge with cheer
Because the GOD of grace who is my JESUS
Always lingers near.

Daniel 3:16-18

Explain line 3 in verse 1.

With reference to the given scripture, expound upon the title.

Consider the Lilies

"Consider the lilies of the field
How they toil and spin not"
Now, what problem do you have
That you think that GOD forgot?

He already knows the things that you need
So trust Him to provide for you as He promised
And do not allow worry to make your
Ulcers develop and bleed.

For you are not being a person of faith
When you allow yourself to be filled with doubt
You should trust in the GOD of Heaven
To always work your problems out.

Luke 12:27
Matt. 6:28

On a scale of 1-10, 10 being optimum, what would you say the speaker's faith level is?

Compare the similarities of the two given scriptures in application.

All I Know

GOD is all I know
I take Him with me
Everywhere I go
If I fall down the steps of despair
When I land at the bottom
I find Him waiting there.

Should I get tossed
Into the pit of gloom
Because He is faithful, He
Reminds me of a special room
That is being prepared for me
Where I can dwell in safety
Throughout all eternity.

So life, your steps of despair
Pit of gloom and your valley of grief
My tenure with, will be brief
Because I have a JESUS
Who watches me and always sends relief.

Psalm 32:7

Give another title to this poem such as, "Bottom Line."

What means, *steps of despair, pit of gloom*, and *valley of grief*?

Situations

When situations in life seem
To have you caught up in a <u>vice</u>
When there is nowhere for you to turn
And trouble sticks to you
Like "<u>white does on rice</u>"
I can tell you true since I have
Been traveling this road for many years
Not to give up on GOD, no matter
The blood, the sweat nor the tears.

Have there been times in my life
When I felt like giving up
Yes sir and yes ma'am, because
Just like you, I don't like to
 Drink from the "<u>bitter cup</u>."

However, I have learned that through
It all, there are lessons that are taught
And lessons that must be learned
And that, because of my commitment to Him
My JESUS will quench the fires of<u> adversity</u>
Before He lets me burn.

2 Corinthians 4:16

Define *vice, bitter cup* and *adversity*.

What feeling tone does the speaker have? Why do you say so?

I've Been Walking

I've been walking with You for many years
Through triumph, heartache, sweat and tears
Yes, most of my life, I have been walking with You
No matter the hurdles I've had to leap
Nor the strenuous paces that life put me through.

I've found that You always do what You
Said that You would
If I but held on and maintained
You worked things out for my good.

Rom. 8:28

Compare and contrast lines 2 and 9.

Expound upon Romans 8:28 with reference to this poem.

Is this poem's title appropriate? Why or why not?

Remember When

Remember when we took pride
In hearing our grandparents say
That this nation of ours was
Christianity based and upon JESUS
We built our faith?

Well, let's not get too far from
The foundation that has been laid
Because, after-all, that faith has
Proven to be tried and true
We just have to stick by His side
And request His help and remember that
He will take of you and me too.

Psalm 144:15

Pull all references to the title out of the poem and expound upon them.

How does the given Scripture apply?

Necessity

Necessity had often been called
The mother of invention
What I'd like to think is that
The "Powers that be" use dire situations
To gain our attention.

I mean, how many times have you found yourself
Between a rock and a hard place
Only to discover that you already had the
Intrinsic tool to solve that dilemma that you faced?

It seems we need to meet our
Challenges head-on, knowing that GOD
Always has a plan
And that He always has His children's names
Written in the palm of His hand.

Psalm 42:5

Define *intrinsic, dilemma.*

What is meant by, *"Powers that be"*?

Give a Scripture for, *"Always has a plan."*

Compose a situation that goes along with the given scripture.

Let Your Gifts Shine Forth

Category 5:

Praise

Not Good Enough

Sarah straightened the last row of chairs, gave the chalkboard a cursory wipe, and went to make a quick trip to the lounge because she knew that the night would be long. Parent Teacher Conferences always were. "I hope that I don't have any troublesome parents tonight," she mused.

Sarah wondered for the *umpteenth* time why the parents of the children she really needed to see never showed up. "Oh well," she thought. "It is what it is."

Sarah finished in the lounge, washed her hands, and headed back to her room. When she rounded the corner, she met her friend, Grace. "Girl, where have you been? You got a whole line of people waiting at your door!"

"What? The doors are not supposed to open until 5 o'clock!"

"Now, Sarah, you know they do what they want to around here and if a parent wants in and if his blood is *blue enough*, he's going to get in."

"Yeah, I guess you're right." Sarah sighed.

"Well, good luck with your parents tonight."

"Yeah, you too."

"Hey, don't leave without me, okay? I don't want to get stuck here half the night with some belligerent parents, you know?"

"Yeah, Grace, I know, and don't you leave without checking with me either."

"Okay."

Sure enough, when Sarah got back to her hall, people were lined up waiting for her. One man made a pointed show of looking at his watch. Sarah put on her best *teacher, hello smile* and invited the first parent in.

The night was going pretty smoothly, with several people just oozing with compliments for Sarah. Several of the parents had complimented her on her expounded definitions, essay tests, and her teaching critical thinking skills to her students. One parent even commented on how Sarah had been able to get her child to like liver and onions, owing to the *recipe* Sarah posted for her students daily. Whenever Sarah posted *liver and onions,* she always told the children that it was good for them. Liver and onions meant that they were having something to do that was difficult and that they generally grumbled about, such as expounded definitions or outlining. If it were something new that was very difficult, she might tell them that the menu for the day was *Brussels sprouts* or *fried chicken livers* with no gravy and no onions. "Haven't had a chance to go by the store and replenish the stock," is what she might say.

Sarah's next parent, the dad of one of her gifted students, was one she knew slightly and liked well enough, which is why what came next was such a shock to her. He started off by praising Sarah for the great job that she was doing with her students. He told her that he liked her innovative way of teaching. He was on a roll handing out platitudes to Sarah. She tried to remain humble in spite of all the lavish praise that he was heaping upon her. Then he said, "It's too bad you're not White."

"What did you just say to me?" Sarah was appalled.

"Well, what I mean is, you are so good at what you do, if you were White, you could write your own ticket!"

Sarah was mortified, but she knew not to let him get anymore satisfaction out of what he had just said to her other than her initial gasping and dropping of her jaw.

Sarah, with icy syrupy sweetness dripping from her voice, said, "Well, sir, I can't help how people see me and what I do. I just do for the LORD and try to let His glory come shining through. That means that when I teach my children, I let what is in the curriculum guide be a jumping off point for me." Her voice trembled with suppressed outrage and shock. "I try to teach my kids life skills as well. Since I'm working for the LORD, that means that I always try to bring my 'A' game, but it's nice to know it meets with your overwhelming approval!"

He held up one hand. "If I have upset you, I'm sorry; that was not my intent. I just wanted to tell you how good of a job we all thought you were doing."

"Yes, and you wanted me to know that you all thought that I was not good enough because I'm not white. This meeting is over." Sarah stood to end the conversation.

Sarah was glad the parent teacher conference was just about over. The rest of the time went pretty much as she had expected. *But what else could have happened after the fiasco of what that man had said to her*, Sarah pondered, as she prepared to leave. She stopped to check on Grace, the scary one, but discovered she had already locked up and gone!

So much for checking on each other. She thought about how happy she had been when she was straightening her desks and laying each student's six weeks' homework packet and progress report on their desk in preparation for the conference. She had been hoping that this conference would not be like some of the others she had had, but that it would go smoothly. She had been so hoping not to have to deal with any temperamental parents throwing fits because she had to tell them about their child's disruptive behavior or about the reason for their child receiving a failing grade in her class. "Well, I got what I asked for. I didn't have to deal with any temperamental disruptive parents tonight. What I should've asked for was a peaceful night, then maybe I wouldn't be feeling so crushed and have my feelings hurt so badly." She thought over her life and about how hard she had always striven to be *good enough to belong.*

When Sarah got home from the Parent Teacher Conference, she was still livid about what *that* man had said to her. She could still hear him in his condescending voice, basically tell her that she was not good enough and never would be because she was Black. "If he could not say something nice, then why say anything at all," she fumed to herself. "At least, that was what her mother had always said."

She could not wait until her husband came home so that she could see his reaction when she told him about it. Sarah already surmised what his reaction would be. He would rant and rave and slam a few doors and threaten to call the man's home. Then he would calm down and vow that that guy had some words coming to him as soon as he ran across him.

Well, his reaction was pretty much what she had figured it would be, except for the mild expletive he uttered, then muttered to himself, "And he better be glad that I'm a preacher ... Insulting my wife like that!"

Sarah calmed them both down and went back into the kitchen to finish up dinner. She surely did enjoy chopping those potatoes for the stew. Guess she was letting off the rest of her steam as she chopped. Sarah thought about how three years ago, she had been approached by a designated member of the Citizens Council. Sarah was told that three teachers names had come up in the Council's meeting as doing an outstanding job, not that it mattered, but two White teachers and her. Sarah would remember that next thing that had been said to her until the day she died. "Because you three teachers are doing such an amazing job, the Council decided to give you each $20,000!" She remembered that her jaw had gone slack and that she could not even say, "Thank you," for couple of seconds. The man then hurriedly explained that the 20,000 would go to the first one this year the second one next year and the last one the third year. Sarah had been floating on air.

A couple of weeks later, Sarah heard the announcement that the first teacher had gotten her $20,000! It was the talk of the town! She could not wait until next year when either she or the other teacher would get their $20,000. She waited and waited but never heard a thing. Toward the end of the second year, Sarah was told, in passing, that the Citizens' Council was not doing the $20,000 awards anymore. When Sarah had expressed her disappointment upon hearing the news, she was empathically told that it was a private group and that they could do what they wanted to with their money. Sarah had always suspected that the other teacher had gotten the $20,000 because her family was very well-connected. She felt that she had not gotten hers because she was just *not good enough* and never would be because she was a black woman.

By the time Sarah finished fixing dinner, she was calm enough to talk about the underhanded compliment that she had been given in a rational way. If he had realized that these remarks would go with her to her grave and be in her mind for JESUS to see as He wiped away tears from her eyes, she wondered if the man would want to take them back … Probably not.

Saying "Your act is great, but you are not because nothing good can come out of you," still hurt.

Then she thought about JESUS and Nazareth and thanked the LORD for gifting her with the skill set that He had. Then she went in to wash the supper dishes and then to grade papers.

That night, before she fell asleep, Sarah came to the realization that there would always be a group somewhere that she never would be *good enough* to belong to because the groups that she would be playing to would be changing over the course of her life.

Sarah knew that one day she would be going to where the chilly winds of racism didn't blow, and all problems would be no more. Sarah fell asleep anticipating another day of teaching her kids the skills with which the LORD had abundantly blessed her.

For Pondering:
What would have been your response if you were spoken down to as Sarah was?

Is that what JESUS would have done?

Did You Know?

Did You know that
Did You know that because…
That I can go on
Of course You did
You know all!

Job 42:2

The theme of this poem is?

Is Job 42:2 a good backdrop for this poem? Why or why not?

Auxilio Ab Alto

I know that if I please You
I will be exalted in Your love
That blessings will rain down on me
Like nectar, from above.

Thank You for giving me the poem
That I just now wrote
For sending it to me LORD, as
To Your throne I spoke.

Thank You for my being a recipient
Of Your amazing grace
Because it takes away all of my fears and doubts
And puts serenity in its place
No matter what kinds of trials I face.

I see Your justice and righteousness
They, like the sun, come shining through
So, I go where You send me
And do what You want me to do
Because I know that wherever I go and
Whatever hardships I see
That Your amazing grace and winged
Protection will continue to sustain me.

Isaiah 50:4
Jeremiah 9:24

Define *Auxilio Ab Alto*.

Which of the given scriptures is best suited for this poem and why?

Song On My Lips

Sometimes on our Christian journey
Life can become very hard
And it seems like the harder and harder we try
The more as Christians, we have to cry

With the uncertainties around us
We don't know what life will bring us to
But as Christians we have to remember that
Whatever life does bring us to
GOD will definitely bring us through.

We can be happy and go lucky one minute
And feel lost and bereft the rest the next hour
But we have to keep the faith and remind ourselves
That the GOD of Abraham, Isaac, and Jacob
Holds us within His power.

So get yourself in check
And pray for faith to be strong
Because the mighty GOD that we serve
Can open your lips and give you a song.

A song that you can sing with
A cheerfulness that is rare
A song that will make your friends
And family alike, stop and stare
To shake their heads and wonder
Because through all of your trials
 you will be tripping right along
As if you had never of care.

Because it's inside me to serve the LORD

Is why you will see me do what I do
And so because of what's inside me
I'll sing this <u>snippet</u> of a song to you.

Since I have gotten older
My voice pops and cracks and will
But the forest would be mighty quiet
<u>If all but the best songbirds</u>
Kept their voices still.

I want somebody to see
 That I keep going, no matter
If I'm laughed at and no matter
How people make me feel
Because I told the LORD a long time ago
<u>JESUS, take the wheel</u>.

And I'm not singing this song
Because I sound so good
But when I am gone, I just want somebody to say
She worked for JESUS while she could.

Ephesians 3:14–19

Define *snippet,* the *bereft.*

Overall feeling tone of this point?

Explain *"If all but the best songbirds keep their voices stil*l."

Explain, *"JESUS, take the wheel."*

DEO

LORD of HOSTS, GOD of eternity
Just want to tell You what You mean to me
Thank You for the trials You brought me through
Thank You for showing me that nothing
And no one else would do.

GOD of Jacob, thank You for enabling me to see
That You are the only One Who
Can fulfill my joy and satisfy my needs
Thank You for allowing me to just be.

Psalm 106:1-2

Define DEO.

Explain this poem against the backdrop of Psalm 106:1-2.

School of Your Love

The relationship that I have with You is rare
And the love that I have found under the wings of Your care
Has allowed me to grow spiritually while there.
I continue to work on, JESUS, for I
Want to be assured of a seat in
Heaven when I get there.

Psalm 54:4

Why is the poem entitled as it is? Use specifics from the poem to support your answer.

Give another Scripture that coincides with the given scripture.

I Clap My Hands

I clap my hands and praise my JESUS
In spite of how you look at me
So I don't know what He has done for you
But I know what He has brought this child through.

I have traveled over many a weary mile
Over much treacherous terrain
He has stayed my fears and guarded my ways
And let the world know that I am His child.

So when I clap my hands
With your looks, don't censor me
For I praise my LORD for all He has done
And will do, on my continued walk toward eternity.

Hebrews 11:13

Define *treacherous, terrain and censor.*

Is the speaker bothered by how the world perceives him/her?

Provisional Love

I woke up this morning at dawn
To a world covered in pristine white
I marveled at what my LORD had allowed
To cover the landscape through the night.

Seeing the squirrels scampering about in
The pristine white covering my backyard
Made me remember my GOD's love
Saw two squirrels sitting eating in a row
In the midst of all the pristine snow
Ah, the bountiful blessings provided by a faithful GOD
Who sits on His throne in Heaven above
And watches the tableau here below.

Deuteronomy 7:9
1 Corinthians 1:9

Define *provisional, pristine, tableau.*

Tie the title of this poem in with each of the scriptures.

Category 6:
Willingness

Being willing to serve the LORD means that I have relearned to be flexible and not to get into too much of a flap about anything anymore. "Looking to the hills from whence cometh help," is what you have to do daily if you have given your life to Him and told Him how willing and ready you are to do His will.

In life, we are often called upon to do things that are just plain hard and to do things that we would rather not. The good that happened to us, we took in stride as life happening the way we had always envisioned that it would. The bad? Now that is a horse of another color. But I had to learn that sometimes we have to wade through the bad times, whether of our own creation or not, to appreciate the good times when they do get to us. Let me tell you a little story.

I got up coming to worship one Sunday morning and the morning proceeded pretty much as usual, you know morning hygiene ritual, breakfast and the usual 40-minute drive to worship, etc. We had a good worship service and after it was over, I had to attend the ladies room. Well, my husband, in the meantime, picked up my stuff off the seat where I had left it and took it to the car, trusting soul that he is...

Yes, you guessed it; he left the car door unlocked and came on back into the building. I exited the ladies' room and started toward the exit since I had noticed that the lights had been turned off. I took two steps and remembered, "Oops, my things still upfront on the seat where I left them," and I turned around to go get them. When I got to where I usually sat, yes I'm guilty of having a favorite seat, like most of you, *(tee hee)* I saw that the seat was empty, so I surmised that my husband had taken my things to the car for me. When I got to the car the front door was ajar. That surprised me, but I found my purse and my black bag that I usually keep my iPad in, thus no problem, right? Wrong! *(But I did not know that at the time.)*

At any rate, we had been invited to dinner at a local eating establishment by one of the members and his wife. We went, had an enjoyable meal and fellowship together and left the restaurant replete. When we got to the car, I went to look in the black bag for my iPad so I could play a quick game of one of my favorite free downloads. I could not find it, so I looked a little harder. Then I realized that it just was not there! My husband, noticing my frantic searching, said to me, "You must have left it in the seat in the building." *(I let him get away with that statement, although I knew that I had not left it anywhere. He was the one that picked up my stuff and my iPad from the seat.)*

So there we were heading back to the building. *Because I was so concerned about getting to my iPad, it seemed to me that the man drove 20 mph all the way to the building. I know that he did not, that's just how it seemed to me.* I told him at one point that maybe he ought to let me drive. He just looked at me as if I had two heads and kept on driving. My stomach was in knots by this time. Well, we got to the building, he got out of the car and went inside to retrieve my iPad. He stayed so long that the first frisson of alarm started to creep up my spine.

I unbuckled my seat down and was getting out of the car when he exited the building with a puzzled and funny look on his face while shaking his head from side to side.

I jumped out of the car and went into the building, my body starting to become cold and methodically calm. I tend to do that when the situation has become dire, only to go to pieces when the crisis is over. *(I have been told that that is the beginning of shock; I wouldn't know, as I'm not a medical professional.)* We looked the building over, high and low, the restrooms, the basement, etc.... No iPad! I kept thinking, "Where is my iPad?"

As a poet and writer, to say that I was devastated by the loss of my iPad, does not begin to cover the situation. The first emotional experience was disbelief, then shock, followed by hurt/pain and lastly anger. I, who pride myself on being flexible and leveled-headed, wanted that person caught and caught right now! I calmed down and then started the notification process that you have to go through when something is lost or stolen. Thankfully, I had engaged a numeric code for my iPad, so that gave me some measure of satisfaction, but not much.

I had been telling someone the day before the theft, about the fact about one of my favorite Scripture verses is Romans 8:28. That Scripture got a workout that week because I kept repeating it to myself. I kept telling myself that, "All things work together for good for those that love the LORD." So to keep from acting like I felt like acting I started praying and here is the prayer I uttered:

Now LORD, I don't know how You are going to work this out, but I give over to Your will for my life LORD. I ask You to help me through this day and all the days and make me be able to graciously accept and work through the adverse things that may happen. Please make my faith grow by leaps and bounds as I learn to depend on You. Prosper my way so that I may use all situations to Your glory. In Your name I pray. Amen.

If you pray a similar prayer during all of your adverse times, you will find that He gradually works things out and that things don't bother you the way they used to. You will find that people start to come to you and say things like, how do you stay so calm in situations like this? Etc. Then, my friend, you will realize what it feels like to have other people watching you and have their faith growing by judging your reaction to things! You might think, "What! Don't watch me! I'm just trying to make it myself!" No, dear friend, you have become a person to emulate. Yes, that is an awesome responsibility, isn't it? Uhm-hu-m-m, but you will get joy and added strength in knowing that your troubles and botherations have, not only helped you, but have helped someone else as well.

"Balderdash," you say? Okay, well think about this for me, will you? Haven't you ever seen someone whose shoes you were glad that you were not in? Someone that you thought to yourself in wonderment and admiration, "He/she surely does have strong faith! I don't think that I could do this or that. Sure you have! We have all thought similar thoughts. Well, you, my friend, have just become that person to someone else! Daunting, isn't it? I know. But you get used to it after a while and then you walk resolutely on, knowing that, "All things work together for good for those that love the LORD." And further knowing that you have to keep moving because someone of lesser faith is looking at you and assessing your reaction and emulating you! And yes, though they don't know it yet, their faith is being strengthened by watching you! Wow! That is really something to wrap your brain around; isn't it?

Remember that I told you earlier in the series that nothing you do is to no avail? Well the scenario that I just presented proves my point that with your every action and reaction you are leading somebody somewhere. It has been said that, "Uneasy lies the head that wears the crown." That simply means that when people look up to you, whether you want them to or not, that becomes a heavy responsibility, but not unbearable. And you never carry that weight alone, if you know the LORD, that is.

When fate finished thrusting me in various situations
I went right back to my childhood training
Into my childlike trust in Him and
That is where I shall stay, come what may
I was unflappable as a child and am again
No more worrying about what's going to come up now
What is coming up for me, I have no idea
But I will leave everything
And His capable hands, that I do vow
Because I have learned through study and the lessons of fate
That He orchestrates my life according to His plan

That He has my name written in the palm of His hands
And that He can handle me and my problems with the swiftness
And aplomb that leaves me awestruck and saying, "Wow!"

So when your journey gets hard and you can't run anymore, walk. If you can walk, crawl! But you keep on praying, crying when you have to, but you keep on going because one day... One day! All of this will be over...

So, put those tears away; pack them up in your tear rucksack. That is the place where I keep my tears that do not want to go away, you know those heartaches that can surface when you least expect them to and shake your soul to its core? I figured that those are the tears that the LORD said He would wipe away.

One day, there will be no more tears, no more pain, no more funerals... When we... "Enter into the joys of the LORD." "For eyes have not seen nor ears heard the joys that the LORD has prepared for those who love Him." W. O. W.!

And you, my friend, have just become the recipient of a care package from Heaven via my heart to yours. Be blessed and be a blessing for nothing you do is to no avail. If the LORD is for you, no matter whatever situation you may find yourself in, you will always do like cream and rise to the top.

Let's talk about that cream for minute. What makes a cream rise to the top, the churning. This can be likened to events in life. Let me explain. Those situations in life that turn your world upside down and turn you all about, maybe your ticket to the top. Think about it. Here's an example, and I go to the good old historical book, the Bible. Don't you know that when Joseph was thrown into a pit by his brothers because of pure jealousy, that it didn't feel good down in the pit? *(Jealousy, by the way, will make folk want to kill you, but that is a topic for perhaps another day).* And don't you know that when he was snatched from the bosom of his daddy to be sold down in Egypt, that it didn't feel good?

By GOD's grace, he landed in a noble's house down there, but trouble was not finished with him yet. He was sent to prison because of an untruth because he would not play ball with his master's wife. Here again, this did not make Joseph feel good. But even in prison, Joseph still had that cream quality. He rose to the top. You know the rest of the story so I will not trouble you with the details. The point that I'm trying to make leads me to my quote for the month which is:

"Keep your chin up, for it all comes out in the wash."

Life Application: What would your response have been if your iPad with all your work had come up missing on a church parking lot, of all places?

Would you confront the person if you were pretty sure that you knew who took it?

Would your confrontation help or harm the cause of Christ? Explain.

Read My Bible

I read my Bible because I was told to at first
But reading the Bible has created in me and <u>unquenchable</u> thirst
And a <u>voracious</u> appetite for feeding from GOD's word
And I'm learning deep things about which I have scarce heard.

1 Peter 2:2

Define *voracious, unquenchable.*

Explain the appropriateness of the title.

Yes, JESUS

…I mean, who would want to listen to me anyway
I cannot make folks be still and listen to my voice
They want to do the things that they want to, for
They are known to do things of their own choice.

Yes, JESUS, I am willing to do what You want done
Though I never thought that *I* would be the chosen one
To carry out Your special plans for encouraging my fellowman.

Yes, JESUS, I will go and do the best that I can
But I don't feel worthy of the task
Because I am just a woman.

Yes, JESUS, You gave me the ability
To be an encourager and a teacher, too
But I am scared that I will fail
And I don't want to disappoint You.

Yes, JESUS, I know that You made my tongue and my intellect
Yes, JESUS, I will listen and learn and keep trying to do Your will
Because You have shown through my living, already
That You will guide me over the rough spots
And help me climb every hill.

James 5:20

What is this poem's theme?

Is the speaker willing? Why or why not?

I Will

JESUS, I will do all
That You want me to do
Because I know that with
Your hand upon me
I can accomplish whatever
You want me to.

I will be an inspirational
Writer, if You so desire
Because I know that You will give me
Whatever words inspiration might require.

I will be a ladies' class teacher
If that is You desire
Because I know that You will help
Me reach the goals to which I aspire.

I will continue to work for You
Even when I tire
For I know that I will
Be with You, LORD, when from
This world I expire
And I am glad to know that Your
Place for me is not the one prepared
With brimstone and with fire!

Hebrews 6:10

What is the theme of this poem?

What is the gender of the writer? Why?

The Coat I Wear

The coat that you see me wear
Is one that my JESUS <u>fashioned</u>
And I wear it with pride and
Display its colors with passion.

The coat that you see me wear
Is one that my JESUS made
It tells you something about my life
And the price for me He paid.

Romans 9:21–23

Define *fashioned* and *passion* in this poem's context.

To expand upon the given Scripture with reference to this point.

DEO Volente

(GOD Willing)

Help me to live so that
Through my daily service
The world can, through me, see You
And see that the tales of
Your lovingkindness are true.

For I am willing to be Your pawn
As I travel this road of life
To ease some weary traveler's load
And to give them rest, encouragement
And a brief respite from strife.

Isaiah 50:4

Tie the given Scripture in with the title.

Name other Scriptures that would fit, as well.

Why for My JESUS

Why, for my JESUS, do
I keep doing what I do
Because He is the one Who
Has always brought me "to" and "through."

Brain Teaser: Give an appropriate Scripture for this poem.

Smiling While Climbing

You taught me how to smile
Through my tears
Taught me how to smile
Through all of my fears.

You dried my eyes and
Stopped their teary flow
You carried me onward, JESUS
Along the route that You
Would have me to go.

Being mindful of the fact that
My spirit, though crushed, was willing
You sifted the soup of my soul gently
To scoop out the kernels of doubt, pain, and woe
That were in my cup of suffering
Which was close to overfilling.

Job 8:21

What physical things can the last verse be likened to?

State the relevance of the given Scripture to the poem.

You Don't Know

"Whatever will be will be."
And I am not apologizing anymore
As to why the LORD has blessed me.

You see, you are looking in from the outside
And don't know my heartaches nor
The rough terrain over which I've traveled nor
Seen the tears that I strove to hide
Just be glad that you are an onlooker
And didn't have to live my life from the inside.

Daniel 6:4

What seems to have been the speaker's lot?

Give another title that could go with this poem and another scripture, as well.

My Life Is Not Easy

My life is not easy and
Hasn't been for some time
I've had to scale many valleys
And had many hills to climb.

But the wonder of it all
Is that I would do it all over again
If it would make my JESUS proud
And to one day say
"Welcome home my child; come on in."

1 Timothy 6:11-14

What does the speaker mean by *"scale valleys" and "hills to climb"*?

Write Your Own Ticket

You say it's too bad that I'm not like you
That I could write my own ticket
If only that were true.

Well, in response to your statement
I'm not working for fortune or fame
I'm just trying to work for GOD
Who personally knows my name

He does not care how much I own
How much "blueblood" I lack
He does love me as I am
And I am not turning back.

So He allowed me to write my own ticket
And I know that surprises you
But take a page of learning from my book
And from now on, be careful what you say and do.

Next time it might not be *little old me*
It might be an angel you're talking to.
Never know…
Now do you?

So we write our own tickets
Yes, that is true
Say, what destination did you spell
When you wrote on the ticket handed to you
Did you write Heaven
What did you write, hell?

Hebrews 13:2

What is the mood of the speaker?

The theme of this poem is what?

How does the given Scripture apply to this poem?

Write a paragraph on your response to this poem if the subject in question had been race? Been religion? If JESUS were literally standing there when you answered, what would your answer have been?

Which Autumn?

Oranges, reds, and shades of gold
Oh, what a magnificent sight to behold
A cloud passed in front of the <u>orb</u>
Less magnificent to absorb.

Why is the poem entitled "Which Autumn"?

Can you see how this poem might have been titled "Which of the Three Autumns"?

Define *orb*. Explain its usage in this poem.

Supply an appropriate Scripture for this poem.

I Get It Now...W.O.W.!

A little evergreen grew beside the road
On a crest, on a rock <u>laden</u> hill
He'd lived there many seasons in
Conjunction with his buddy, the
Oak, who lifted his branches high in the sky
As if he wanted to touch the clouds
If a low one should pass by.

He kept his arms extended as though in praise
No matter the change of the seasons
"Don't you get tired?" the little evergreen said
"Why don't you just rest your arms
And not always keep them raised?"

The oak, who rarely spoke a word, replied with a sigh
"I have to keep my arms lifted in praise
In case mankind comes by
Because they are not strong like me
And need to be reminded that JESUS died.
They have to see things being constant
Though life often brings changes
"What are you talking about
I don't understand what you mean."

Listen little one, you are
Part of the plan as well
Why do you think you were
Allowed to remain forever green?
It's so that mankind can be reassured
By your continual never changing
Just like my raised arms tell them that I will
Remain constant though seasons come and go

Let Your Gifts Shine Forth

It is to remind them that we are born to die
And the changing of my leaves remind them
That seasons are a part of the life that we know.

But my continued raised arms remind them
That GOD, Himself, has <u>orchestrated</u> a plan
That, though hard times come, is
Constructed to always take care of man.

"Oh, now I understand what you are talking about
You are saying that, no matter what happens in a man's life
He needs to keep his arms lifted in prayer
Because GOD is mindful of him and uses my being evergreen
And your changing leaves to remind mankind
That He is constant in His care."

My being evergreen is a reminder that GOD is always the same
And your changing leaves are a reminder that
Situations come and situations go
But your constant outstretched arms are a reminder for mankind to remember
That about, a praying man, GOD will always know!
I get it now.
W.O.W.!

2 Timothy 2:13

What meaning does this poem seem to be trying to connote?

Explain how the given Scripture applies to this poem.

Define *laden, orchestrated.*

Category 7:

Encouragement

Today, I want to talk to you about encouragement. I discovered several years ago, a passage in the Bible that has resonated with me ever since. That passage is Isaiah 50:4. Basically, the passage says that, if you have the gift of being an encourager, it did not happen by mere chance. It says that, that gift is to be used to help your fellow man who may be weary from time to time.

This is a gift that I have been given to use and I use it to the glory of GOD. So, when people want to tell me their problems I listen. Why, because it is part of my makeup and part of my life's journey as an encourager to "Do What I Can While I Can." You know, there are some simple joys and some simple gestures of love and care that I get immense pleasure out of receiving. So, I figure that if I like them then maybe somebody else will too. So, I use some of those tactics as I go along on my journey, trying to be an encourager for the downhearted.

When we were children, we used to be told by the old folks that were living in our happiest days and that we'd better enjoy them. I did not understand what they meant then. I used to think to myself, "Best days my foot! These ain't no best days, being spanked at someone else's whim." *(Ha ha)* I can laugh at that simple childhood thought now. And I'm sure that you have discovered, just like I have, that those were indeed the best days. I remember thinking that I could not wait to get grown and get my own place. *(Aha ha ha)* Ah-h-h life, it is a good teacher, no?

But you know, one of the other lessons that they taught us guided us when we got our first place of our own and continues to guide us still. What lesson is that? The lesson of JESUS and His love, that's what. We were told that if we leaned on Him everything would be alright. And so, like good students, we did and still do just that. But you know, it seems like when life finds out that you're willing to lean on the LORD, that's when trouble sometimes want to set up shop at your address. It's during times like this that we need encouragement. That's why the LORD, in His infinite wisdom and love, put Isaiah 50:4 in the Bible. And I'm glad that He put that in the Bible because it reminds me that GOD is still in control, and you know we need reminding of that sometimes, don't we? The presence of that Scripture says to me, "Now I know that you're going to get weary sometimes in doing your work for Me and I know that you will tend to forget that I care. So this Scripture is to remind you by its very presence, that I planned ahead for these times and I am having this written down so that you will know that I thought way ahead about you. The death of My Son tells you that I love you. Isaiah 50:4 just reaches forward in time and underscores it! You be encouraged; I have everything well in hand."

When I was diagnosed with diabetes several years ago, I was devastated! I felt bereft and abandoned. Then I wondered, why me? You know how we tend to have a little bit of a pity party for a minute or so when we are given news of that sort. But my pity party didn't last long. Having always been a firm believer in GOD, I took this problem to Him like I had done for so many things throughout my life.

So, to those of you who are coping with a new unwelcome diagnosis or whatever difficult storm you may have in your life, let me assure you that life can go on. Read your Bible to call to mind the numerous times that the LORD has come to His children's aid. You will remember Daniel, the Hebrew boys, and Joseph to name a few. Space and time will not allow me to talk about all the times in the past that He has come to the aid of His children. Just know that He will.

But often times, it's not as simple as that; is it? Because if you stay in a storm for a long enough time, it starts to become your normal. You get accustomed to the battering that you receive from whatever source, and you take it in stride as much is possible. But you know, even when you get hardened to that particular storm, it seems the adversary always hits you with one better. You might find yourself reeling, might find that your resolve has begun to falter. Here is where the words of one of my favorite songs comes into play. Now get this, **just when you had given up hope and practically thrown your hands up in the air because your confidence just wasn't there**; just when the enemy had been trying to convince you that you cannot stand, the LORD comes through and takes your hand. You begin to *see the sun peeking through the clouds* and your o*ne more sunny day* begins once more. You start to think about *those simple joys that you used to know*, and as I was talking about earlier, your step begins to get a little brighter. But I'm a believer that everything happens in life or reason. So when your storm is just about over and it's not as hard for you to smile as it used to be, use that time to uplift somebody else. If the LORD has brought you out of the storm, then you want to, "Brag on GOD," *Power for today, July 2012*. Give somebody else hope to go on by the telling of your story. Help somebody see that GOD is still in the delivering and prayer answering business and that He is faithful as He said He would be. 2 Timothy 2:13.

Empty Arms

A message from GOD is being sent to you
To tell you that He knows the pain
That you have been through
To tell you to keep your faith and never doubt
That JEHOVAH JIREH will work all things out.

To tell you that when your
Situation has been resolved
That you take the time and patience to
In other Christians lives, get involved.

To tell you to pass the message of hope forward
To believers in like situations
Who live their lives in accord
With the will of JESUS
Though they don't understand
To ask you to say, "Just trust in His providence
And hold on to His hand."

Remember to remind them of Jeremiah 9:24
That you understand and trust Him
Because He has solved insurmountable problems
Like this, many times before.

 Dear heart, make no mistake about it
You will be called upon to witness, it's true
And then you can testify as to the goodness
Of GOD and how wonderful
It felt when He brought you through!

Jeremiah 9:24
1Peter 1:3, 6, 22

Define *providence.*

What is the mood of this poem?

For what purpose was it written?

Is the speaker talking from first-hand experience? Substantiate.

Why is this poem entitled, "Empty Arms"?

Counseled Many
(for Brendell)

You have counseled many
And have helped the <u>tottering</u> to stand
By strengthening <u>weakened knees</u> and
Fortifying <u>weakened hands</u>.

You have done a great job
And have done it with <u>finesse</u> and care
And the LORD will reward you
When you climb that <u>celestial</u> stair.

But, I just wanted to tell you that
You are appreciated for all that you give
I just wanted to give you some of your
Flowers while you, yet live

Rom. 16:3-16

Define *tottering, weakened hands, weakened knees, finesse,* and *celestial.*

What is the general mood of this poem? Cite from the poem of evidence of your conclusion.

The Book

Romans chapter 15 and verse 4 reads
"For whatever things were written aforetime
Were written for our learning, that through
Patience and through comfort of the scriptures, we might have hope."

This verse tells me that GOD is
And has always been, mindful of man
It further says to me that He cared
Enough about me before I was born, to
Have had words of comfort, for me prepared.

That verse also tells me that I have to
Learn not to rush Him, but must learn to wait
It further tells me to trust in His timing
For He never shows up too late.

When I see, in my mind's eye, Daniel come out
Of the lion's den, without even a scratch
It tells me that the GOD I serve
Does not have an equal match.

When I read about the giant, Goliath
And how David brought him down
It reminds me not to worry about my enemies
Because my JESUS's love always surrounds.

There are many other stories that can be found in
 The pages of the Bible; you just have to slow down
Enough to read what has been placed within.

Again, a reminder for you to stayed prayed up and
To go back to the book

Where you can find solutions to all of life's
Problems, if you would, but take a look.

What is the overall message of the poem?

What is the theme of the poem?

What is the speaker's faith level, on a scale of 1-5, with 5 being great?
Substantiate.

Alma L. Carr-Jones

You-u-u Who-o-o!

You-u-u Who-o-o!
Yes, it is you I am talking to
Girl, I have been yard "saleing" too and let me
Tell you about a deal that I just found
His name is JESUS and
He is the best deal around,

Honey, He knows about everything
That I have ever done
But He still loves me girl
Because He is GOD's Son.

He said that He wanted
Me to work for Him
Though my past was shady
And my future *(without Him)* looked grim.

So I am goin' to tell it
Everywhere I go and
To everyone I meet
Because the payday that He
Is giving is, too-o-o sweet
And the deal that He is offering
Just cannot be beat.

You better come on *chile'*
And get you some of this
Because this is some good stuff
That you don't want to miss.

Well, *gotta'* go, but I had to tell somebody
And it was good meeting you

Hey, give me your number and
I will holler back at you.
… You-u-u-u Who-o-o-o!

Acts 5:42

Why is the poem entitled as it is?

What is the general mood of the poem? How do you know?

What does *shady* mean in line 13?

Does the speaker know the person spoken to well? At all? Why?

Propensity for Loving

I have a propensity for loving
That makes me be kind and giving
And it is something I will keep on doing
As long as the LORD allows me to keep on living.

You see, He has not stopped loving me
So I won't stop loving and I hope, neither will you
Because I am made in His image and trust
Him with all I have and with all I do

I do have one question before I am through
Are lovingkindness and giving, an integral part
Of your life; what can you answer fellowman
What does your life say about you?

Corinthians 5:14

Define *propensity* and *integral*.

Explain the appropriateness of the title to the scripture.

Good Enough

By this world's standards your
Efforts might not be good enough
But there is a Higher Power
Who sees below the surface
Right to the core of the heart
Who sees each man's merit and worth
Who judges men with justice
And never gets the horse before the cart.

So, your efforts, while small in man's eyes
Should be made to please the LORD
Because He knows what you are all about
And will judge your efforts with like accord.

Hebrews 6:10

Where does the speaker seem to place the merits of physical beauty?

Has the speaker ever been judged harshly? What makes you say so?

How does the given Scripture correlate with the title of the poem?

Alma L. Carr-Jones

Happenstance

In any new <u>quandary</u> in which
You happen to have been thrown
Look for similarities to past experiences
That you made it through and
By which you have grown.

You will find that fate, though <u>fickle</u>
Will often toss you a limb
That you can grab a hold off
Depending upon your whim.

In any new circumstance, always
Learn as much as you can
Because you never know when you
My need to draw upon your past
To tackle new jobs head on and
To perform accompanying tasks.

1 Peter 5

Define *happenstance quandary* and *fickle*.

How does the title relate to the category of Encouragement that this poem has been placed under?

Stormy Trials

You know what I figured out
About the stormy trials that we face
They move us out of our comfort zone
And put us in a strange, <u>quirky</u> new place.

In the book of Matthew, chapter
14 and verse 30, we see
That Peter, who was safe on the boat
Asked the LORD to let him come to Him
He trusted in JESUS to keep him afloat.

Old Peter did well, I must say
Because he managed to walk on water
For a minute or so, anyway.

Then he took his eyes off JESUS
When he saw the raging storm he was in
And, you know, that is something
We often do, as mortal men.

We weather our storms pretty well
Until the gale gets rough and
The seas start to swell
Then we do like Peter and take
Our eyes off JESUS
Then we cry aloud
"LORD have mercy
Please save me!"

As I said before, storms and trials
Take us out of our comfort zone
But I can stand with assurance and say

That my GOD can handle any adverse situation
That happenstance should send my way.

Define *quirky*.

With 5 being the greatest, on a scale of 1 to 5, what level of faith would you say that the speaker has? Substantiate.

Heaven Is Listening In

When Heaven is listening in
On your conversations of life
Be careful what you wish for
You may be granted something you <u>abhor</u>.

When Heaven is listening in
On your groans and complaints
You may get an early call
To be a departed saint.

Just take what comes to you
As your <u>allotted</u> due
Work through whatever circumstances you're in
And keep going until get through.

Don't wish your life away, but
Be thankful for the dawn of each new day
And remember, Heaven is listening in
So be careful of what you might say
Because you might cause yourself to miss
Some blessings that were headed your way.

In short, Heaven's listening in
Is something that happens all the time
So walk with surety, whatever your lot
And keep your <u>faith steeping</u>
In the <u>believer's simmering pot</u>.

Could keep going with this poem
But you by now, get my drift
Just thought I'd do both of us a favor
And give our spirits a lift.

James 5:10-11

Define *abhor, allotted.*

What is meant by the phrases, "*faith simmering*" and "*believer's simmering pot?*"

Expound upon the message of the poem and tie in the given scripture.

Bene Feeling

Have you ever gotten the feeling
That good things were coming to you
Because of the havoc that life
Has wrought, that change was long overdue?

Ever had the feeling that things
Were about to change because you
Kept your faith against all odds
That your blessings had begun to accrue?

Have had that feeling several times of late
It made me euphoric and giddy
On the inside and for the good stuff to
Happen to me, is an impatient wait.

1 Thessalonians 2:16

Define *bene, havoc, accrue, euphoric* and *giddy*.

What is the general mood of the speaker?

Category 8:

Christian Life

Mrs. Ruby Saga 1

Awoke this morning to the sound of Mrs. Ruby calling my name on the creative channels of my mind. She is a heroine in my latest story. I planned to do a quick story on her about giving up when life gets hard and then I had planned to move onto another piece. Mrs. Ruby, it seems, is not content to go quietly off into the sunset of her debut story. She intends to be around for a while. So with that said, it is into the throes of Mrs. Ruby's misfortune we go to see what escapades she and I find to get into while she wrestles with her waning faith.

As we enter her story, we find that she is a mighty disheartened lady right about now … "What happened to cause her faith to become shattered and weak?" is probably what you're asking yourself. Well, let's delve right back into our story. This is where we will take up in the life of Mrs. Ruby.

Everybody in the neighborhood loved Mrs. Ruby. No one ever had an unkind word to say about her and her neighbors were decidedly bothered about losing her. However, their being bothered did not begin to cover how Mrs. Ruby felt about it herself.

Here she was getting ready to move to a nursing home after giving a life of service to the LORD and to the neighborhood. She has to leave everybody that she has known most of her life. Ruby had not felt this bereft and alone since her mother died back when her son, Matt was seven years old. Ruby had always loved the LORD and He had always taken care of her. That was why Mrs. Ruby could not believe that something would not happen at the last minute so that she would be able to stay in her own home surrounded by longtime friends and her church family. Still as moving day got closer and closer, her hopes began to dwindle.

Mrs. Ruby's yard was one of the showplaces of the neighborhood and had always been, as far back as most people could remember. She was proud of her yard and deservedly so, as she had once remarked to her friend, Gladys from down the street, "I don't have anything else to keep me busy now that I'm retired. Matt has married and moved to Minnesota and Sam, bless his heart, has passed on."

Ironically, it was the yard, or her meticulous care of it, that caused Mrs. Ruby to have to give up her home. How could the yard lead up to her having to give up her home? Well, here's the way it went. She and her husband, Sam, had always kept their yard immaculate, but with his passing, that left Mrs. Ruby to do both of their jobs on the yard or let it go. She opted, at first, in memory of her Sam, to keep the yard as immaculate as it had always been kept. Then, she decided later to keep it up because she liked doing it and it occupied her. Even when the doctor told her to wear a hat and spend no more than two hours a day out in the sun and despite Matt's scolding, she had doggedly decided to keep her yard. She did condescend wearing the straw bonnet, though. Yet, she stayed out in the sun for about four hours every day.

On this particular day, Mrs. Ruby had just finished planting her north flowerbed and was planning on doing the big bed in the back on Sunday and putting the finishing touches on the east bed on Monday. She was walking around to get a good look at a few last-minute touches that she needed to do to that bed when she tripped over a roller-skate that one of the kids had left in the garden path. Mrs. Ruby grasped at the air and tried to catch hold onto some of the young saplings, all to no avail. Down she went. *(Woof!)* She awoke to sirens screaming and people in white peering over her. Mrs. Ruby realized that she was in the emergency room at the hospital in Junction Town. She knew that because the hospital and Scuttersville, her hometown, did not have the pretty little nurse trainees in the pink and white striped uniforms. It was too small.

Ruby remembered that the last thing she saw was the broken sapling that had come away in her hand when she tried to stop herself from falling when she tripped over the skate.

"Oh well," she thought. "Time to give this cart to someone who really needs it." Having said that to herself, Mrs. Ruby went to vault up off of the cart. When she did, she screamed with pain and fell back limp in a dead faint. What she did not realize and didn't find out until later was that she had sustained a mild concussion and had broken three ribs when she tripped and fell.

She fell folks, but not to worry, she's okay, basically that is. She is a little bruised, has a mild concussion that the doctors want to watch and has three broken ribs, but as she is often fond of saying, "One tide does not a beach washout."

Now spiritually, Mrs. Ruby is not faring as well. She keeps wondering why the world has turned upside down and nobody up there is listening to her anymore. She is wondering what she has done to make all of this happen to her. Folks, have you ever felt like Mrs. Ruby's feeling right now? How did you handle your situation?

Well, at any rate, she has her son, Matt, and me. We are ever by her side, but that does not seem to be enough for her. She is reaching for something deeper. She has become listless and has developed a defeatist attitude. That bothers me because, if you knew Mrs. Ruby, you would know that giving up just does not *cut the mustard*, according to her that is. Why, she is the one who, by talking about the benefits of prayer, brought me back from the brink of despair! She taught me that in this life, prayer allows us to shed our fears and place our problems, which to us sometimes seem insurmountable, into the hands of Someone more capable than we are of handling them.

I will keep you posted on her struggle with her faith; in the meantime, if you know a Mrs. Ruby in your life, pray for her and extend whatever kindness it is in your power to bestow. You could be setting the backdrop for your own future, you never know, reader; you just never know.

Here is a poem that I wrote for all the Mrs. Rubys of the world:

Don't despair
No matter what you're going through
Begin your day with prayer and peace of mind
It's what you will find.

He will take a load from your heart
That you thought you could not bear
And leave tranquility resting there

He is the MASTER of all things
Tangible, abstract and surreal
Lean on Him, dear lady and
Experience the peace that only He
Can make you feel.

She is a sweetheart but a little bit of a fussbudget since she fell. Bless her heart.

LORD, You Are the Potter

LORD, You are the Potter
You created me
LORD, You are the Weaver
Who fashioned the mantle that I wear
LORD, You are my everything
And I thrive under Your care.

Isaiah 64:8

What is the overriding theme of this poem?

Explain the theme in at least three sentences.

What Did JESUS Do?

What did JESUS do for me
He eliminated my past
And illuminated my future.

1 Tim. 1:15-16

Explain *eliminated* and *illuminated* in the context of this poem.

Give another title to this poem.

When GOD Gave Us JESUS

When GOD gave us JESUS
He gave us His very best love
Who are we to decide that
We don't have to please Heaven above?

...You see, He makes sure that the
Things that I need, I don't lack
I cannot speak for you, but
I just want to love Him back.

2 Corinthians 5:14-21

Explain the relevancy of the given Scripture to this poem.

Reduce verse one down to one word in meaning and verse two, the same.

Now, build your own poem, using the two-word framework that you have built.

Measuring Stick

Don't use your past life
As your measuring stick
Instead, use what the LORD would have
You be and to that <u>precept</u>, try to stick.

In short, don't say, "I am not what I ought to be."
This statement might subconsciously say to you
I can still "live" a little; I don't have to strive
Just yet, for <u>impeccability</u>.

Revelation 22:13

Define *precept* and *impeccability*.

Why is the title aptly chosen?

Would, Should, Could

Some of the things that we
Would do, we don't do
Some of the things that we
Could do, we won't do
And some of the things that
We should have done, we can't do.

Hebrews 13:15-16

Explain the essence of this poem.

Work

He has exposed me to it
Why does He have to beg
To get me to do it?

For, one day the opportunity to say
Yes, will be withdrawn
And we will be judged by what
We have said and by what we have done.

2 Thessalonians 3:5-7

Is there an impending message to this poem? If so, what is it?

Make application of the given Scripture to the phrase, "Yes, will be withdrawn."

It's Not About

It's not about the diamonds
Or about the rings
It's about the love of GOD and
The joy that His love brings.

It's not about houses, land
Or other acquired things
It's not about power such
As wielded by kings.

It's about living for GOD
And honoring His glory
It's about telling this world
The age old story
Of how JESUS died on that old tree
So that we could live with Him
Throughout all eternity.

Luke 12:15

Construct a poem on "What It **Is** About."

Will Not Bow

Will not bow, bend, nor burn
No matter what life does to me
It will not make me turn
My back on goodness to become
At advocate of pain, disillusionment and duress
I'm stepping on folks through my pain
And waiting for opportunity, prosperity and fortune
To knock on my door again.

For I know a man named JESUS
Who cares for me now
And it does not matter at all
What you do, old enemy
For my standard word of operative performance
Has now become "W.O.W.!"

Psalm 40:5
Deuteronomy 4: 34
Psalm 77:14

Explain the title.

Explain the essence and application of the last line of the point.
Tell a story of your own using one of the given scriptures.

Alma L. Carr-Jones

I Know Where I Am Going

I know where I am going, so
It doesn't matter where I've been
I just want to ask you to
Look at what He did
He took a lowly nobody
To gain the world's attention
He's using me to tell my fellowmen
To rid their lives of sin.

Not saying that I am perfect, for
That is far from being true
He just chose to use a like vessel
Who could identify with you.

Matt. 5:14-16

What is the mood of the poem?

Is the speaker humble? Brow beaten? Why?

Make No Mistake

Make no mistake about it
I am not tough
Because the road that I am traveling
At times, gets mighty rough.

Still I find that I am
Made of sterner stuff
Because each hurdle that I leap
Makes me toughen up
Though each mountain that I climb
Makes me huff and puff.

But I don't fret and I don't worry
Because I have a hidden <u>ASSET</u>
Who comes whenever I call
I have a hidden ASSET
Who will not let me fall.

So, you say that you don't know
What I am talking about
I'm speaking of the GOD of Heaven
Who's always waiting to be asked
To help His children out.

If you haven't gotten to know Him
Then it is not too late
Because you will need His protection
To block the blows of fate.

What to do to find Him
Is no mystery at all
You just have to hear the gospel

And then obey its call.

When you believe, repent, confess
And then be baptized
Then you are His child, as you
Probably have already surmised.

But your journey does not stop there
That is not its end
You have put down your old life
For another one to begin.
Then you must study your Bible
So that you can grow thereby
And you have to pray each day
And, in faith, know that your
JESUS is always standing by.

1Peter 1:7
Job 23:10

Define *asset* and *surmise*.

Give a Scripture for the lines that are underlined in verse 4.

Which of the two scriptures given, is a better fit for this poem and why?

A Christian Life

Trying to live a Christian life
Can be kind of tough
For enemies hit you with troubles and strife
And all kinds of unpleasant stuff.

But I am glad that I
Serve a GOD Who decides when
My enemy has done enough
And can take my enemy and show him
That his stuff is not so tough.

Psalm 27:3

What is the general mood of this poem?

Has the speaker had trouble with enemies before? Does the speaker
know anything about deliverance?

"Touch Not"

It does not pay to bother a person
That the LORD has put His mark upon
For He will engage you in battle
And you will have nowhere to run.

You see what He did to Egypt
When they bothered the Israelites
After their tangle with the LORD
They tried their best to take flight.

It did them no good to run
For they had already stirred Him up
His fury was unfurled and they had
To drink the wrath from His bitter cup.

Psalm 27

What is the theme?

Explain the given Scripture in reference to the poem's title.

Warrior GOD

In spite of the heartbreak
That I have been through
You never let me fall, but
Kept me closely <u>coddled</u> to you.

And no matter what calamities on me befell
You sustained me JESUS with your strength
So that I could lift my eyes
And say, I am doing well.

And when everybody thought that
I was out of the fray
You stepped in to say, not yet
She will live to fight another day!

And about the winning of the battle
It's not mine about which to boast
Because the victory belongs to You, LORD
Jehovah NISSI, LORD OF HOST!

Exodus 17:8–16

Define *coddled.*

Give two other scriptures that epitomize the title of this poem.

Who Is She and Why?

Who is she and why
Do you care about her
She is just a penniless, powerless nobody
…but she is a penniless, powerless nobody
Who is loved and treasured from on high.

Listen little one and let me give you a fact
Sometimes the people we belittle
Are placed in our path for a reason
Maybe it is just to test your reaction
Maybe it is to see if you, like most
Will treat them with contempt and
Add to your list of "oops", yet another infraction.

Whatever the reason people are
Allowed to cross our paths
It doesn't cost us anything to be kind
It doesn't cost us anything to care
Because we'd want like treatment if
We should find ourselves walking there.

Matt. 7:12

What is the message of the poem?

Who is being spoken to?

Memorize the given scripture.

Whatever

I am a work in progress, but I have
Learned that it is not about me
That the LORD utilizes me how He wills
To do His work that is set forth for me
In whatever capacity that I can fill.

I have to be flexible
And use whatever talents I have
To help spread the gospel
So that its message can be heeded.

1 Timothy 6:11-19

Why is this poem's title very apt?

Alma L. Carr-Jones

The LORD Can Bless You

The LORD can bless you wherever you go
Is a fact that I can say for sure that I know
You see, I traveled to North Carolina to
Work on the Obama campaign
And owing to His thoughtfulness
I was brought to astonishment once again.

I had always wanted a machine on which I could serge
But I never had the money that I felt
Like on a machine I could splurge.

My JESUS placed me in a home
While working on the campaign
With a loving couple who had a serger
That she was not going to use again
She made a gift of the serger to me
In addition to her generous hospitality.

There I was in North Carolina among
People that I did not know
Working and laughing and having a good old time
…Just goes to show you
He can bless you anywhere you go.

Jeremiah 23:23

Define *serge* and *splurge*.

What is the poem's theme?

What is the mood?

What is the level of faith of the speaker on a scale of 1-5? Substantiate your conclusion.

Any Given Day

Don't understand all the "whys"
And "wherefores" of life but He
Who loves me, tempers all of my struggles
And carries me through my strife.

So, I can go where I need to and not be
Concerned about what's waiting for me there
Because I have a loving JESUS
Who shelters me with His care.

Do you know Him, brother,
And you, sister, too
Have you gotten to know His love
And experienced the joy in knowing
That His arms of protection surround you too?

1 Peter 1:5

Substantiate your determination of the theme and faith level of the speaker in this poem.

The Killing Frost

The killing frost touched the trees and made
Them bring forth their various hues
And in like manner, touched the apples green
And their vibrant red did ensue.

What would happen fellowman if
The killing frost decided to touch you
Killing frosts come and killing frost go
But aren't you glad that you can't
Be "touched" unless He says so?

Psalm 78:47

Expound upon the title to the tune of, at least, eight lines.

What is the message of the poem?

Soul Speaking

Soul of my neighbor said to
Mine, "I like what I see."
Said my soul to my neighbor's
"Come on over fellowman and follow me."

I am on my way to a land
That has joys that the half
Of, have never been told
I'm on my way to that land
That Isaiah spoke of, in days of old.

1 Corinthians 2:9

Expound upon who is doing the speaking in this poem.

Prove that the title can be correlated with the given scripture.

My Community

I wonder, in my community
What my neighbor sees
When he looks at me.

Does he see a committed Christian who
Displays the light of JESUS as he should
What is the word about me
Around my neighborhood?

Have I done things to make my
Community a better place
Does my fellowman see my discipleship
As I run this Christian race?

Can I be seen reading my Bible as I
Rest in my patio chair
Have I shown hospitality and invited
My neighbors over for simple fare?

Just a series of things I
Have wondered about
Just wanted to check myself as
I live for the LORD and try
To carry His plans for my life out.

Luke 11:33-36

After figuring out the mood and theme of the poem, make an
application of and correlation to the given scripture.

Who's Looking?

Boy, pull your pants up
You don't have to be so tough
Have some dignity about yourself
Take some pride in the strides made for you
Step up young man, because enough is enough!

Keep your dress down young lady
There's a whole lot of living yet to be done
Don't believe all the sweet nothings
Whispered in your ear because
A lot of sweet nothings turn out
To be *true* sweet nothings, you hear?

Old woman, stand and act your age
Your life is about over and
You're on your life's last page.
What have you built with the life
That you were given
Can people see from your life's journey, the work
For Him, for which you have striven?

Smile old man; don't be so bitter
Show the church of tomorrow that
You are persevering and that
You are not a quitter.

In summary folks, make the most of each day
Because you never know which pair of eyes
Just happened to be looking your way.

Matt. 5:14-16

What is the theme and mood of this poem?

Is a warning implied? What did you base your conclusion on?

Thousand Dollar Talk

To have a "thousand-dollar talk and a ten cents walk" ...
Must remember that we are "epistles read of men"
And yet, talk is so cheap
Because you are measured by what men
See you do, so whatever promises you do make
Remember to do your best to keep
And always mind your *p's* and *q's* because
Whatever you sow, so shall you reap.

2 Corinthians 3:1-3
Galatians 6:7

What is the message of the poem?

What old saying can be applied to this poem?

Make a Difference

Make some plans for making a difference
In the lives of somebody else, the motto of
"Doing What You Can, While You Can"
Should be an integral part of your life
And cause you to be "soul" aware of your fellowman.

Gal. 6:10

Prepare a two-minute speech on the importance of the essence of this poem.

Because

Because He cared(s)
He shared(s)
Made in His likeness
Because I care
I share.

Ephesians 5:1-2

What is the theme of this poem?

To See the Holy Land

If I got the chance to walk
The Israeli countryside
If I got the chance to listen
To the tour boat guide
I wonder what impressions would
Be placed upon my poetic mind
I wonder what I would glean
From the experience
To share with man and womankind.

Whatever impressions, if any, I might receive
I guess we'll never know because
To the Holy Land, alas
I don't have the currency to go.

But then again, I might be
Like many other tourists
That have traveled along these routes
I might not garner anything except
To have an exciting trip
But, it would be the experience of a lifetime
Of that, I have no doubt.

Amos 9:15

Does the speaker have a yearning for something?

How does the title of this poem correlate with Amos 9:15?

Category 9:
Sin and Confession

Mrs. Ruby, Saga 2

"Well, it has all come to this," thought Ms. Ruby. "Me doing my memoirs over a life almost spent. Well, it won't be as long as it has been. That's for sure," she thought as she settled herself in her new recliner chair that someone had brought to the nursing home expressly for her. She didn't know who. Someone was always doing something nice for her, but always anonymously. Ruby didn't care though; she was just thankful. She remembered how apprehensive and reluctant she had felt about moving to the nursing home/assisted living center up here in Idaho.

She had to move to Idaho because her son lived here and wanted to be able to see her and check on her. Lands-a-mercy! She never lacked for visitors that's for sure. If it was not her son, it was her grandson and his girlfriend, or one or two of the church members. Ruby guessed that, as these places go, this one was not bad at all. She had nursing care when she needed it, especially with when to take her meds. That, she definitely appreciated. Plus, having a car was a rarity in this place, so she was often sought out for girls' trips. So much so that she had had to designate Wednesday as the only day she would drive her group around town. They all chipped in on the gas though and gave her a piece of change now and again. *All in all, not a bad deal.*

Mrs. Ruby was so glad that she had her own little two rooms and a bath. The place, roomette, as Ruby liked to call it, was tiny but she liked it well enough. When she visited some of the other rooms, she felt like a celebrity. Take her friend, Minnie, for example. She was in a room with a woman who barely spoke or interacted at all. That was hard for chatterbox like Minnie.

All her friends knew, firsthand about Minnie's loquaciousness! Her saving grace was that she kept them all in stitches with her stories, whether real or made up! Minnie was definitely a character. They all told Minnie that she ought to write a book, to which Minnie replied, I would miss my next story while trying to write one down! They all hooted with laughter.

Mrs. Ruby stood up to position her pillows just so behind her back and when she did, she slipped on the rug again, fell back, and hit her head. When she realized where she was, she was lying down on the floor with her arm at an odd angle. She could not maneuver herself to get up so she pushed the call nurse pendant that she always wore around her neck. She had not wanted that dreaded dependent on her neck getting tangled in her hair, but her son had insisted. She was glad now that he had. Her son! "Oh, mercy me," thought Ruby. "He would be a worrywart for sure now!"

Her arm was starting to throb now… The intercom buzzed in her roomette. "Hi Mrs. Ruby! What *cha* need?"

"I fell down and I hurt my arm. Can you… hello, hello…" Ruby's roomette door flung open and two burly looking men and the little charge nurse came running in.

One of the big burly men, who Ruby later learned was named Joe, looked at her and said, "Aw-w, she's all right! Much to do about nothing, if you ask me." Joe grabbed Ruby to stand her on her feet and her left arm flapped backwards limply. She screamed and fainted. Mrs. Ruby awoke in a dazed state and went to rub her arm and the movement made her notice the IV in her right hand because it hurt.

"Great!" thought Ruby. "These things always hurt me!" She then noticed that she felt sleepy…*(z-z-z-z)*

"There was something wrong. What was it?

Oh yeah! That man had hurt her arm when he jerked… Her arm? It was in a cast! And there was writing all over it. She could hardly see the cast for the many signatures on it. Ruby was starting to feel sleepy again. She thought can't go to sleep. *Gotta* look at the room and… When Ruby awoke she noticed two things:

The overwhelming smell of flowers and stuffed animals and balloons! Wow, she thought. Somebody sure got a lot to deliver! She drifted in and out of sleep and woke to a darkened room with the bedside lamp as the only light. Ruby thought, "I need to go to the bathroom."

"Okay, Mom I'll help you sit up and then I'll call the nurse," said a voice from the shadows in the corner of the room.

"Matthew, is that you?"

"Yes Mom, it's me."

"Well, I don't need no nurse to go to the bathroom. You just help me to the door."

"Can't do it, Mom. That Dr. would have my head if you fainted and hurt yourself again. They told me to call them and that is what I'm going to do."

The door swung open briskly. "Okay you ready to eat something, Mrs. Ruby?" said a spunky young nurse with dreadlocks.

"Might want something to eat if I can get to the bathroom first."

"We can do that for you, Mrs. Ruby. How is your arm feeling baby?" the spunky young nurse asked.

"Ain't no baby and my arm hurts like wildfire. No thanks that big idiot that jerked me up off the floor."

"You don't worry about him, baby. I will get you something for the pain okay?"

"Okay," said Mrs. Ruby.

After Ruby had settled back into her bed she said, "What happened to that big *fella* who jerked me up so fast?"

"Don't worry about him. He won't be jerking nobody else anymore. He's lucky he's not locked up!" said the nurse.

"And still might be!" growled Matthew.

"Do you mean you got fired, him with children to feed here in the dead of winter!" Mrs. Ruby started to cry; just then the doctor walked in.

"What's going on in here, Matt?"

"Aw, she's upset about the guy losing his job after only one day on it. She'll be all right, Doc."

"I'm hungry!" said Mrs. Ruby.

The doctor told the nurse to get her some food STAT. The nurse said okay and started out of the room. Mrs. Ruby's crying got louder and became caterwauling! She wailed, "I'm hungry but I aint *gonna* eat until you get that big buffoon in here who jerked me up. And I want him in here now."

"I don't think that would be such a good idea, Mrs. Ruby, what with all that has been going on and all," said the doctor.

"Now, Mom," began Matthew.

"Don't you 'Now, Mom' me, Matthew Granger. I know what I'm about. When I fainted, I went in and out of consciousness and I heard that poor man screaming about how sorry he was. He said he never meant to hurt me. He fair begged to keep his job and you went ahead and fired him anyway. You get him in here now, right now!" A pause hung in the air. "Then, I'll eat."

The doctor threw his hands up and said that he had to make a phone call and the spunky little nurse wanted to take Mrs. Ruby's blood pressure and temperature. Mrs. Ruby glared at her and said one word, "No!"

Really must've dozed off again but then she dreamed she smelled fried chicken, Chinese food, catfish, chicken and dressing… She smelled everything it seemed that she liked. She just lay there with her eyes closed just savoring the smells from the vivid dream she had had. She knew that they would be gone when she opened her eyes.

"Mom?"

"Matthew," she thought.

"Better eat some of this before it gets cold."

It wasn't a dream. There was laid out on the table in her room everything that she liked. All her favorite dishes, even sweet potato pie. She looked at it and started to cry. She looked at her son and said, "Matthew, I'm so hungry. I want to taste it all. But I can't. I got to know that that big fellow has his job back so we can feed his children." *(sniff)*

"Mom, he has his job back, well… almost. He is a bit clumsy and strong, so they gave him the job of head janitor, not patient care orderly. He is very thankful just to have a job. He said that that was what he did before his mom's sickness caused him to relocate."

"Yum!" said Mrs. Ruby. "Matthew, please cut me a tiny piece of that pie and a chicken leg and…"

Mrs. Ruby ate until she could hold no more. *(burp)* "Excuse me," she said.

As Mrs. Ruby drifted off to sleep, Matthew had a question, "Mom?"

"Uhm hu-m-m?"

"How did you hear him pleading for his job? That happened way down in the director's office after you had already been taken to the hospital."

"Don't know, Matt. Maybe I dreamed it. Don't know. But I know that my being a Christian just wouldn't let me cause him to lose his job. I just couldn't do it. I just couldn't do it!"

Matthew pondered over the strangeness that his mother was known to have from time to time. As he watched his mom's chest gently rise and fall when she succumbed to sleep, he chuckled to himself, "A good meal always did put you out didn't it, Mom?"

Safe Haven

You asked me how it felt to
Leave the church and go
To wherever this world called me
And my wild oats to sow.

Well, listen to a contrite and broken spirit, please
Who tells you as a friend
Stay in the church; stay in the church
And your soul, He won't have to mend.

For this world is full of shadows
That you know nothing about
And it's better to dwell in happy innocence
Than to find some "home truths" out!

Hebrews 6:18

What is meant by *home truths?*

Why is the poem entitled as it is? Cite examples from the poem to
substantiate.

Baring of the Soul

The baring of the soul is
Something that makes you feel great
For you can continue on your journey
With a lighter load and a cleaner slate.

I can get forgiveness
For any wrongs I have done
And I can keep striving for perfection
For, my clean slate means
That my sins are none.

Isaiah 43:24-26

What does the title of this poem mean?

The Bottle

(A Shape Poem)

The
Bottle
Messed
Up My
Life
Because
The
Bottle
Cost
Me My
Wife.
Sorry Baby.
1 Timothy 3:3
Proverbs 23:21
I'm a changed man now.

This is an example of shape poetry. What wrong does it portray?

Write a shape poem and portray a wrong with it.

(Senryu) on a Sinner

Road smoothed out ahead
For a changed sinner like me
See what has been done.

1 Tim. 1:15-16

Make an application of the given Scripture to the poem.

Me Again

Hello JESUS, it's me once again
Coming before you in my unworthiness
To acknowledge and ask forgiveness of my sin.
Am so thankful that You
Love me in spite of my sin
Am so thankful that You
Accept me again and again.

Psalm 103:11-13

What is the mood of the poem?

What is the faith level on a scale of 1-5 that is portrayed in the poem?
Substantiate.

GOD of Mercy

To the GOD of all mercy
To the GOD of all grace
Thank You for loving me anyhow
Though I often fall on my face.

Thank You for forgiving me, LORD
When I find it hard to do so myself
Thank You for Your marvelous love
And for saving my soul from death?

Rom. 4:7-8

Give another Scripture for this poem.

JESUS

JESUS, I have sinned against
Heaven and against Thee
I am trying LORD to be
The best that I can be
But LORD, I know that I
Am not at all worthy.

But owing to Your grace
And to Your phenomenal love
You keep encouraging me to press onward
Even if I move at a snail's pace
Toward that blessed home above.

Ephesians 1:7

Define *phenomenal.*

Dissed

Thank You LORD because Your love for
Me made You override the shame
Of being slapped and <u>dissed</u> in front of men
In <u>reciprocal</u> LORD, the love I have for You
Allows me to do some of the same.

John 18:22

Define *dissed* and *reciprocal*.

The Answer Is

The answer is
No, don't bother
Not interested because
I serve the JESUS.

No to the "joint"
No to the "drink"
No to the club
And no to the dance
Because I have given my life
Over to the LORD and on missing
Heaven, I'm not willing to take a chance.

Rom. 6:23

What is the message of this poem?

Who is being addressed?

Is the speaker bitter? Why or why not?

"Ain't" Gonna' Stop Trying

I "ain't" gonna' stop tryin'
No matter what you do to me
Yes, I see you gloatin' over the
Tear stains that are evidence of my cryin'.

Well, just you be careful how you rejoice
Over the havoc that you have wreaked for me
For you may be sowing an entire field
That has to be reaped by you **and** your posterity.

Micah 7:8, 10

Is there an implied threat in this poem?

Alma L. Carr-Jones

Cleaning Up Messes

Cleaning up messes that you make
Can be harder than you think
Because some messes in life, expand
Much farther than the kitchen sink.

Soap, water and degreaser will cover
Most messes that you make in your kitchen
But please, forgive me, made a mistake
Are often, from conversations, missing.

Matthew 18:22

What is the message of the poem?

This poem can be likened to what?

Wrong Done

Going around and having ill will toward someone
Is not going to accomplish anything
So why not let bygones be bygones
And maybe a soul to CHRIST, you will bring.

Remember, it is not about the wrong
Done to you or to me
It's about a Heavenly habitation…
A place to spend all eternity.

If someone has wronged you and
You can't get over the deed
Just do what JESUS did and
See a soul in need.

You have had to be forgiven
For things you've done yourself
They why do you feel justified
In withholding that blessing from someone else?

Col. 3:13

Define *habitation*.

What is the theme of this poem?

Alma L. Carr-Jones

If You Had Known

If you had known that He loved me
You would not have trifled with me
If you had known that He counseled me each day
Cruel man, you would have let me be.

Somewhere I read, "Be careful
How you treat strangers: you may
Be communicating with angels unawares."

So be careful how you treat your fellowman
For, Somebody's watching and Somebody cares!

Hebrews 13:2

Define *trifled*.

Does the poem carry a warning? How so?

Explain Hebrews 13:3 in application to this poem.

Wonder Why

When the storm came up and it started hailing
Wonder why you came running to me
You cannot possibly manage to feel safer
Around a "too prayerful" person like me.

You, who had just been ridiculing
Me for my devoutness
Came into my room and wanted to make small talk
You are lucky that I am trying to
"Make my calling and election sure"
Because, if I weren't sister, I would have
Told you to, "Talk your small talk and walk."

1 Peter 4:4

What is the mood of the poem? The message?

Expound upon the underlined section in the last verse.

Fishing

A fish caught too small or of the wrong type
So glad to know that He won't throw me back
No matter if I disappoint Him, for
Forgiveness, He will allow me to
Remain a part of His catch
And continue to build in me
The character traits that I yet lack.

Hebrews 12:5-9

What is the message of this poem?

Kept On

Thank You, LORD JESUS, for the fact
That You kept on fishing until You caught me.
I, in turn, keep on looking for that day
When I see You coming back
Then all of our hopes will be fulfilled
And our joy will be intact.

Mark 14:62

Is the poem aptly titled?

Does the poem correlate to the given scripture?

Final Judge

When people make mistakes
As humans are prone to do
It <u>behooves</u> us all to remember
That we make mistakes too.

I can't say that I never made a mistake
That just would not be true
I just get up, dust myself off
And keep trying, to GOD, to be true.

I try to live my life to please
The Being who dwells inside of me
For He is the final Judge
Of where I will spend eternity.

2 Peter 3:3-4

Define *behooves*.

What is the theme of this poem?

7 Days

If seven days were all the time
On earth that I had left
I would work non-stop to get all of my
"Meant to" things off of the "forgive me" shelf.

I would be on fire for the LORD and would tell
Everybody I met to get their life in accord
With the way that the LORD wants us to live
I would talk repentance to liars and adulterers
And tell their wives/husbands that
They needed to forgive.

I would read my Bible every spare minute
Of the day
And remind my children/spouse
That JESUS is the way.

I would let them see and hear me praying
As I tried to live the life to back-up
What I was saying…

If you had seven final days given to you
Are those some of the things that you would do
What about the homeless, the prisoners and the sick
I bet that the problem of neglected Christian duties
Is one lollipop that you would try to lick.

If we would do all of these things
If we knew we only had seven days
Then what is to keep us from starting
To change our slothful ways?

2 Corinthians 5:10

What is the theme?

What is meant by the "*Forgive me shelf*"?

R-U-Ready?

The intention was to do it
But Death came before
I got to it.

Revelation 22:12

Explain the given scripture.

Alma L. Carr-Jones

Category 10:
Heaven and Eternity

Ms. Ruby Saga 3

Mrs. Ruby seemed to spend her time dozing, reading her Bible, and entertaining visitors most days and daydreaming vivid dreams most nights. She only got in short naps during the day because someone was always dropping by to say hello and/or to ask for prayer.

She still looked forward to her visits with her grandson, Beanie (Benjamin, as he insisted that she call him now, but to her he would always be Beanie). She had finished her memoirs and they had sold well enough, so well, in fact, that she had been able to give Becky and Beanie both trust annuities of $150,000 each.

She still smiled each time she saw her son, Matthew, with this middle-aged man spread beginning to manifest itself in his little bit of a rotund tummy. Her Matthew had been going it alone since Kaitlyn's death due to a hit and run driver four years ago. They never found the driver, but Matthew had made his peace and gave himself totally to his plastic surgery practice and to the church. Her Matthew, an Elder! Who would've thought?

Mrs. Ruby sleeps and dreams.

"Hey! Nana! Yeah, it's me Becky! It's good to see you looking so well. Nana, you know I have never been able to keep anything from you, not that I would want to anyway, but I wanted you to be the first to know that I am pregnant with twins. Seth and I are so excited!

I've started going to twin parenting classes and Seth has already been interviewing for live-in nannies. Me, I don't know how I would feel about another woman in my house unless it were you or Seth's mom.

225

You wouldn't consider moving Down Under would you? A sweeter nanny I cannot find other than you, Nana. Thank you for being you all these years. Love you and see you later. Oh yeah, love the new pink satin slippers and since when do you like bells on your shoes? *(Tee hee)* They are cute, though! Bye!"

Mrs. Ruby awoke to the sound of the meal trolley in the hall and to the subsequent jostling of her food tray as the peppy little charge nurse brought her food in. Behind her came Matthew and Beanie and Beanie's girlfriend. They made their entry with a rounding chorus of "Happy Birthday."

Mrs. Ruby was aghast! She had forgotten her own birthday! She chuckled gleefully as she said, "Mercy me! How can a body forget their own birthday?"

Beanie said, "It's not for you to remember, but for us, Nana, so we can show you how special you are!"

Matthew chimed in, "Exactly!"

"We brought presents!" said Beanie's girlfriend.

"And Chinese food," said Beanie.

"Don't forget the fried chicken and sweet potato pie," piped in Matthew.

Mrs. Ruby chuckled as she noticed the charge nurse eyeing Matthew.

"Matthew, things are looking up around here." She nodded toward the charge nurse, who was blushing profusely. "Wouldn't you say so, son?"

"Well, Mom I guess so… No, I would definitely say so," he said, while grinning at the charge nurse.

The charge nurse reached over and removed Mrs. Ruby's cafeteria tray from her bedside table to make room for the food brought in by Matthew and Beanie. When the nurse returned from the food trolley in the hall, she said, "It looks like we're going to have a full-blown party with the entire family here!"

At that Mrs. Ruby said, "Not the entire family, for my granddaughter, Becky, could not be here, not physically anyway."

Matthew and his son, Beanie, looked at each other as if to say, "Oh boy! Here we go again."

Mrs. Ruby, with a chicken leg in one hand and a slice of pie in the other, took a bite of pie and said, "Good pie, who made it and Matthew why didn't you tell me that Becky was expecting twins?"

Matthew hollered, "Because I didn't know that's why!"

Beanie yelled, "Say what!"

"Mom, with that new iPhone, you keep up with everybody faster than the rest of us can," said Matthew chuckling.

"Didn't need no iPhone, thank you very much," said Mrs. Ruby.

"Then, how…," said Beanie.

"Had myself a dream that's what," said Mrs. Ruby.

Matthew and Beanie said in unison, "Oh, a dream…"

"Yes, to both of you, I did, and I saw me some hideous pink slippers with bells on them, too. Everybody knows I don't want no tinkling bells ringing every time I take a step telling everybody I'm coming before I get there. 'Course the slippers were satin and I did like that."

"Uh, right, on all accounts," said Beanie's girlfriend while reaching for a pink and white polka dotted package.

Mrs. Ruby, egg roll in hand said, "Go on and open it for me, honey. You *gonna* be family anyway."

Matthew and his girlfriend gave each other looks that said, "How'd she know?"

And Matthew said, "Nana, can we have at least one surprise for you?"

"Don't know if you can or not, but not with the pink shoes and not with your ring for your girlfriend and not you know what."

The charge nurse chimed in with, "Oh, now who's blushing?" They all had a good laugh.

Matthew said, "Well I'll be! When were you going to tell your old man, Son?"

"Well, Dad ..." The door opening interrupted him. "Becky! When did you get here and how..."

Becky put her purse on the table and made a beeline for Mrs. Ruby. Laughing, she said, "It's called hopping a plane with your husband to see the best Nana in the whole world wide world!"

Ms. Ruby squealed, "Becky! My Becky," while holding her arms out for a big hug, eggroll and all.

While hugging Becky, Mrs. Ruby whispered to her, "I know about the twins, but when will you know if they're identical or fraternal?"

Becky, who had gone limp in Mrs. Ruby's arms, had to recover herself.

"Nana, you can't just spring stuff on me like that. I'm expecting!"

"I know you're expecting, and I also know that you are carrying the knowing inside you, too. Always have had, but it only shows itself when the current carrying family member is preparing to move on.

"No, Nana. No!" said Becky.

"Now, no carrying on, you'll upset the babies and we don't want that, do we?" said Mrs. Ruby.

Beanie said," Aw-w, Nana!"

Matthew said, "When?"

"Not before I get to help the twins blowout the candles on their second birthday cake.

It'll take me that long to get Becky used to her gift of the knowing," said Ms. Ruby.

Matthew, you will be marrying the charge nurse here and Beanie, you will have seven daughters, one of which will have the second seed of the knowing and you will be governor in New South Wales one day. You rascal, you, Matthew! I didn't know that you had stock in opal mining! Will wonders never cease!"

Three years later…

Mrs. Ruby looked forward to getting up today. As she waited for her longtime nurse/friend Nancy from her assisted-living days, she glanced out the window. She looked forward to riding Matthew's daughter Minnie and the twins Pansy and Pinky on her scooter as they tore down the main corridor of the house, out to the wraparound porch veranda. Such opulence, such happiness and her great grandbabies… Such joy…*(z-z-z-z_____!)*

When Nancy came in fifteen minutes later, to help Mrs. Ruby get dressed, she found that her best friend was gone. And she had been left all alone.

Angel Wings

Ms. Ruby had climbed
The celestial stair
To find Sam waiting there.

Hand-in-hand they
Went to see
The Savior who had died
For all humanity.

One day we all will
Have to do the same thing
As we pull off mortality
And don Angel wings.

Almost Done

My time of working in the
Garden is almost done
And I wanted to tell you something
I have found to be tried and true.
When life gets hard sometimes
Let me tell you, hon
That faith in GOD and persistence
Will pay off for you.

John 5:28-29

What is the faith level of the speaker? Substantiate.

What is the message of the poem?

This poem could have fit well in which of the other sections in this book. Why?

Lovingkindness

Shining through the window
Of an early morning
You made me take pleasure in
The fact that I was born.

Your playing the slats
Of the Venetian blinds
Caused your ever present lovingkindness
To be brought again to my mind.

Your beams overshadowed everything in view
Oh, to have been able to travel onto the beams to their beginning
Would be a trip worth taking
If one were assured of winning.

What is the theme of this poem and what is the message?

What is the mood of the poem? Substantiate.

Provide a Scripture for this poem.

Thank You, Bless You and Praise You

Thank You for the qualities upon me that You have bestowed
That enable me to bear my burdens, re-shift,
And to carry my heavy load
As I make my way Home
Continuing to climb Heaven's road.

Thessalonians 4:16

What is the mood of the speaker?

Is Your Insurance Policy in Force?

Back in 1987, we suffered a debilitating loss
Fire robbed us of all our worldly possessions
But due to rising insurance costs
We had switched to a cheaper company
And that there was a one-week lapse
In coverage is a sad but true confession.

We play similar games with our lives when
We sin and act like there is no tomorrow
We are setting ourselves up for heartache and for sorrow
GOD has already shown us how He feels about sin.

In short folks, I am going to rely on Him even when
I have to go through those "even though" times in life
Because folks, when I approach Heaven's gates
I want to hear somebody say,
"Alma Jones, come right on in."

2 Corinthians 5:1-10

What does the underlined phrase in the last verse refer to?

Write a brief essay to explain the title, essence of the poem and correlation to the given scripture.

Some Sorrows

There are some sorrows, even when you pass them
That you carry with you to the grave
But as mature adults, we have learned
To keep stepping on because
We have learned how to behave.

Having never carried a baby under your
Ribs is one such sorrow, I vow
But I keep going in spite of it
Because this world is not my home, anyhow.

When I get home to be with my JESUS
What has happened to me down here
Will not matter in the least
For I will live with no more sorrow
And never shed another tear.

Revelation 21:3-4

Define *vow.*

Substantiate the mood, message, and theme of the poem.

Very Blessed

Very blessed is how I see my life
Yet, I've had my struggles
And, yes, I've had my strife.

Very blessed is how I see my life
For it is the avenue through which
I must travel to make it to
That Heavenly abode
Which is being made ready for my habitation
All I need do, is stay on the Heaven-bound road.

Hebrews 11:16

Define abode and habitation.

What is the theme? Could there be a secondary theme?

Heaven

The love of JESUS made me decide
That it was Heaven that I wanted
So I pursue it with a zeal and
With a fervor that is undaunted.

Though by this world
I am often taunted
I have a meeting with JESUS
That has already been appointed.

By the HOLY SPIRIT
I have been anointed
And I am making my way
Heavenward, undaunted.

1 Thessalonians 4:16-18

Define undaunted.

What is the message of this poem?

GOD's Gonna Take Me Home

If you see me cry as I try to do my JESUS's will
If you see me struggle as I take my walk up trouble hill
If you hear me moan, as I go along my way
Just know my dear brother and my sister
That GOD's "gonna" take me home one day.

Then all the struggling for me will be o'er
And I'll join saints from bygone days
Upon that celestial shore.

Revelations 21

What is the mood and the theme of the poem?

Touch of My Master's Hand

Something I understand is that one day
My MAKER will touch me
With His powerful hand
And all of my tears will be wiped away
And with the hosts of Heaven
I will get to stay.

Revelation 7:17

Write a paragraph depicting the scene presented in the poem.

Will Finish My Stint

I will finish my stint with time
And begin my sojourn with eternity
To dwell in that blessed city where
There is a mansion prepared for me.

Ephesians 1:3

Define stint and sojourn.

What is the mood of the poem?

Last Tomorrow

When you hear of my demise
Don't weep for me with red rimmed eyes
For I go home to be with JESUS
And I go with a winning smile.

No more pain, worry nor sorrow
I've said goodbye to my last tomorrow
For I go home to be with JESUS
And I go with a winning smile!

Psalm 116:15

Is the speaker a person of faith? How do you know?

What is the speaker's mood?

What is the time of life depicted in this poem?

Does this poem correlate with the Scripture that has been selected for it?

See You Later

For me, it is finished, my
Job of aerating the soil of souls
Has been relinquished
I've moved on
I go to take my rest
See you on the other side, church
Meet me in the land of the blessed.

2 Tim. 4:7

Define relinquished.

Who is the speaker?

Explain 2 Tim. 4:7 in relationship to the title.

Journey's End

I saw weariness and care
Worn across your face
But coupled with that weariness, I saw
Peace and serenity resting there.

You had a long trip in life
Of that I am much aware
But when you reach your journey's end
You will find Him waiting there.

Ephesians 1:3

Who is the speaker?

How can you ascertain the speaker's faith level?

What is the time depicted in the poem?

What is the mood of the poem?

JESUS

Please receive _____, another one of us
That will soon be gone
Over to the other side
Look upon his soul with mercy and joy
And bid him, welcome home.

This poem is written in the form of a prayer about what?

Who is the speaker?

Find a Scripture for this prayer.

Time to Go

Since we were born
All of us know
That one day the call will come
And then it will be time to go
Some, such as yourself, know
The manner and the time
Others of us, just know we
Have to leave someday
But we don't know
The time nor the way.

One thing about knowing the way
And the appropriate time
Our minds naturally go back
To our childhood days when
The love of JESUS was a taught fact.

We have known all of our lives
That one day we would meet
At the end of this life's journey
And our Savior we would greet.

Since you know the time
And there's no denying the cause
Let's take some serious moments
And think about Heaven, let's pause.

I know your sainted mother
You don't want to leave
But son, think about the way
That you leave her to grieve.

Let Your Gifts Shine Forth

Grieve she will, as any mother would do
For she thought the natural thing
Was that she would receive
The call before you.

Since you know that
She will definitely cry
Give her the sweet hope of
Seeing you in the by and by.

 As a child, if you used
To sing songs of praise
Then fix your mind on JESUS
 And with some of those songs raise
Your voice to your Savior
Like you did in your youthful days.

There's nothing so bad
That you could do
That the loving arms of JESUS
Couldn't reach out to save you.

Think about your (daughter, son, niece)
And greet them with a smile
Let them know that you are
At peace with JESUS and let
Them see you in your last days
Brimming with hope and looking
Toward that last trump with style
Because you have sung your last song
And you walked your last weary mild.

Tell your family not to grieve for you
Tell them to get and stay with JESUS
And that you hope to see them on the
Other side when their living down here is through.

Now that you have taken care of
The things you needed to
You can look forward to the day
That the angels come to get you.

Build a two-page essay on this poem and include scriptural references.

Heading for That Rise

I'm on my way home with joy in my step
I'm getting closer to my journey's end
It's the thought of Heaven that has always kept
Me plodding on through many a storm and contrary wind.

Joy quickens my soul; I'm headed for that rise
For when I get to the top of the mountain
I'm headed to a meeting in the skies.

You can't stop me now; I'm on the run
My struggles are just about over
And my race is just about won.

It was hard scaling valleys and climbing high mountains
But hallelujah folks, I can see the waters
Of that great crystal fountain.

All I have to do is climb this last hill and then I'm home
Glory to GOD, folks, the angels are coming to meet me
To show me that I'm not alone
Move over enemy; you can't stop me now
I see the wonders of glory
And all I can say is, "W.O.W.!"

1 Corinthians 2:9

Craft a going home journey as you imagine it might be. Give a
scriptural reference.

Alma L. Carr-Jones

Ultimately

As a young person when
I first went to college
I knew what my life was about
I knew what I wanted to be
I had my life plans all laid out.

I knew the number of kids
That I would, someday have
I knew the type of home
That I would someday buy
For I had grabbed life by the tail
And I was reaching for the sky.

What I didn't realize was
That it was not all about me
It was about my life Planner
The GOD of all eternity.

When I wanted to go left
But had to go right
I shrugged off the inconvenience
And kept my well laid-out
Plans within my sight.

When I tripped and fell
While running my race
I picked myself up, dusted
My knees, and wiped my face.

I kept skipping along
Though I had to hobble now and again
I kept moving toward my dreams
Though sometimes, I was too winded
To sing my song.

By the time I had climbed
A few mountains and labored up some hills
I began to wonder to myself
"Hey! Wonder what's up; what gives?
For this is not the type of life
That I had planned to live."

Then I thought about Jonah
From the Bible days
Who had not wanted to do
GOD's bidding; who wanted to follow
His own ways.

But that was Jonah and
I am me
Besides the GOD of the Bible
Does not have special plans for me.

He deals with superstars like David
Daniel, Elijah and the Hebrew Boys
He does not bother with folk like you and me
Who have always been free to do
Whatever we enjoyed.

Then why are all these things
Happening to me
An elderly neighbor said to me one day
"You are not your own boss
JESUS has the final say.

Plans were made for you
Way before you were born
You have to take your faith in your hand
And begin your GOD-planned sojourn.

You see, Jeremiah 29:11 says that
The LORD does have plans for you

So baby-girl just you wait and
See where He leads you to."

Yes ultimately, He has the final say
I'm just glad that He gives us time
To change our planned route
According to what His plans say.

Though this day be filled with
Chaos and storms
I know that this page is but one
From the plan book that was
Written before I was born.

So, I'll not worry about what's coming ahead
Because just like the lilies of the field
And the sparrows of the air
He has always kept me clothed
And has always kept me fed.

I'll just lean on Him because, ultimately
He cares for me; I know
Because He finished this story
Of mine, a long time ago.

Ultimately, ultimately
What a word; what a word
One of the most beautiful words that
I have ever heard.

So, I would not change one step of
My journey as I found the path for my life
I'll just hold on to "ultimately" and say…

🎶"Ultimately, oh-h-h ultimately
Ultimately, oh-h-h ultimately
GOD has a plan, a plan for me

And the name of that plan, I call "Ultimately." 🖊

Alphabetical Index

NUMERICAL INDEX

About the Author

Alma L. Carr-Jones, a beloved educator, poet/author, a retired educator and a motivational speaker, lives in McKenzie, TN. She is a successful author of nine books to date. Alma loves to write because, as she is fond of saying, "It is something I was meant to do."

She is:

- An Avid Inspirational Daily Blog Writer at: www.almacarr-jonescorner.blogspot.com/
- A Highly Acclaimed Retired Teacher of 30 Years
- Author of Nine Books
- A Preacher's Wife of 40 years
- A w.o.w. (woman of work for the MASTER's use)

This Christian lady is one who really tries to live up to her motto of "Doing What I Can, While I Can." Since she is quite busy doing whatever her hands find to do, that old saying of *wearing out instead of rusting out* will be true of her. She says she wants to have made a difference in the lives of her fellowmen and to have built a legacy that will still speak, even after she is planted in the ground.

To have the treasure of this woman's work in your home is to have a loving dose of life as viewed from the eyes of a preacher's daughter's daughter and the wife of a preacher. This woman has a heart of gold with arms big enough and ears tender enough to help any soul stay encouraged as they make their way toward Heaven. Alma is such a jewel of a woman that she says, when you see her doing something that you admire, "Don't get it twisted; it is not me, but the glory of GOD shining through me."

Other Books by the Author

The Tallest Mountain Series

Get Yourself Up

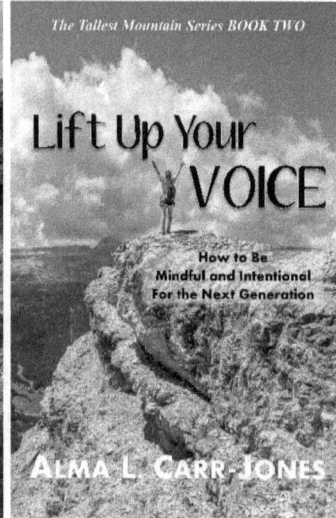

Lift Up Your Voice

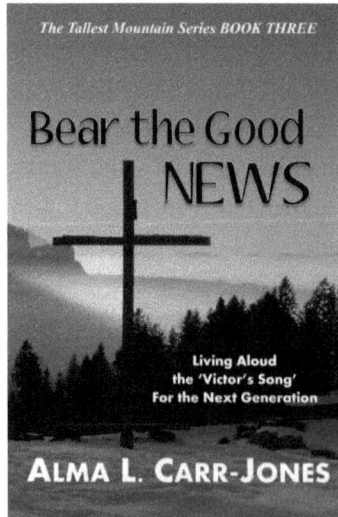

Bear the Good News

Available on Amazon and from the Author

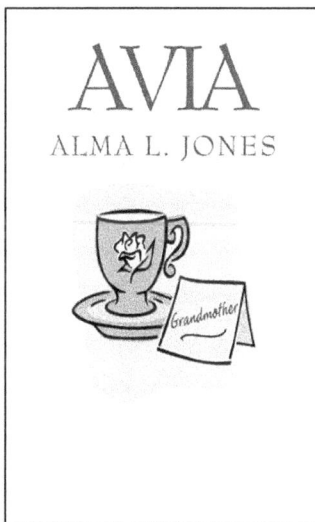

Bonus Poem on the Next Page!

Little Church in Camden's Black Center
(Eastside)

We lift our voices and live our
Lives to Your glory and Your honor
We praise You, JESUS, for Your tender
Love and for Your <u>omniscient</u> power.

The sinful things that I used to do
I don't do anymore
And if You ask me why, I'll say
"I gave my life to JESUS CHRIST; I
Live and work for Him each day.

I have changed so, today I have sent the old life out
And have ushered a new one in
I just want to remind everybody
That I have finished to begin.

I can't believe that I wasted all this time
But I have finished the old
Life that I used to live
To begin my life anew, because
The time that I have left
To JESUS, I freely give.

I want my name to be written there and so do You
So don't live your life like it is all about You
Because what matters when living down here is through
Is what is written in the book about your service
About what chores you were willing or not willing to do.

Through my gardening, hunting, and fishing
I serve and share

To show that I give my life to the LORD
And about my fellowman, I do care.

Today is the first day of the rest of my life
Already set in stone are the events
That have gone on before
Yet, I am mindful of judgment day
When time will be no more.

So brothers and sisters, since that's what it is all about
We need to try to work for GOD and to leave no good deed undone
And continue our sojourn, until we walk this world no more
Then we will be welcomed inside of heaven's open doors.

Where we will lift our voices
In eternal praise to Him
As we bask in His eternal love
And talk with the angels and
Explore our new home above.

2 Corinthians 5:15
2 Corinthians 6:3

Thank you
for reading our books!

Look for other books
published by

www.TMPbooks.com

www.TMPbooks.com

*If you enjoyed this book
please remember to leave a review!*

www.ingramcontent.com/pod-product-compliance
Lightning Source LLC
Chambersburg PA
CBHW072340090426
42741CB00012B/2860